Pressure Canning Cookbook For Beginners

1000+ Days of Essential Canned, Jammed, Pickled, and Preserved Recipes to Affordably Stockpile a Lifesaving Supply of Nutritious, Delicious, Shelf-Stable Foods

Himers Rilte

Table of Contents

Introduction

Canning is a perfect way to preserve and store your vegetables and fruits while they're in season, and it makes your bounty last throughout winter when seasonal and local food items are in short supply. When you enjoy the food yourself, you'll know exactly what you're eating. You can be sure that the food was of high quality and fresh. You'll also enjoy foods that are free of harmful preservatives and additives.

This cookbook explains the process of pressure canning food with easy-to-follow directions. It will teach you the basics, including how to fit the process into your busy life, the equipment you'll need, and step-by-step instructions for pressure canning. You can enjoy wholesome recipes for canning fruit, vegetables, meat, soups, sauces, and so much more.

Throughout the course of this book, you'll learn everything you need to know, from how canning works to what pressure cans should be used. You'll also learn many details about using the right foods and ways to get the most out of your canning experience. By the end of this book, you'll have everything you need to start canning and fill your kitchen with pickled, delicious, and nutritious food.

Chapter 1: Canning Basics

History of Canning

Since longer prehistoric times, humans have tried to develop a new technique to keep their food last longer. At that time, they develop various methods like pickling, drying, salting, and smoking food to keep their food lasts for a long time.

Canning is one of the most popular methods that help to preserve food for a long time. The food is processed and packed into airtight containers which help to increase the shelf life typically from 1 to 5 years and in some circumstances, it is preserved for a very long time. For example, canned dried lentils are found in the edible state after 30 years of a long time.

During the period of Napoleonic war (1803) Napoleon Bonaparte realizes that his soldiers were starving due to lack of fresh food because fresh foods are decaying during the war period. To find the permanent solution on food preservation Napoleon Bonaparte offered a reward of 12000-franc to those who find the cheap and continent way to preserve a large amount of food for his army and navy soldiers.

Nicolas Appert is young chief accepted this challenge and doing long research over food preservation and finally, in 1809 he found that the food cooked inside the sealed jar did not spoil for a very long period of time unless the jar seal was leaked, and food is exposed with oxygen. In Nicolas Appert method of a jar, sealing allows preserving soups, vegetables, dairy products, fruits, juices, syrup, and jellies. In 1810 French minister awarded Nicolas Appert for his experiment. Before 50 years Louis Pasteur explains the science behind sealing. When the food is heated in bottles or jar the microorganism in the food is vanished and the sealing protects food to enter any microorganism enter into food.

In 1810 instead of bottles and jar tin-coated irons are used and patented by Peter Durand. He also supplies a large quantity of canned food to Navy and army soldiers. In the 19th century, double stem technology is used to manufacture most of the modern can. Today the advanced water bath canning and pressure canning technology are used to preserve the food long-lasting.

Why Pressure Canning?

Pressure canning is used to kill harmful microorganisms from food by heating food more than boiling water temperature. Pressure canning is used with food whose pH value is higher than 4.6 such food is also known as a low acid food. There are many reasons using pressure canning some of the reasons are as follows.

- **Saves your time and money**

If you are growing some vegetables and fruits into your garden and your freeze is no more space, then you can use pressure canning technique to preserve your food you can also use extra meat to preserve it properly. This will help you to save your money. It not only saves money but also saves your time also because most of the canned food is ready to cook. You never need to soak beans or defrost meat before cooking

- **Preserve lots of food at once**

Using a pressure canning method you can canned 15 to 16 jars at once this means you can lots of food at once. If you find a good deal over meat or your favorite turkey, then also using the pressure canning method you can store lots of food at once.

- **Canned food supports you during a hard time**

If you are facing tuff time like job loss, hard economic time, critical medical conditions. Canned food is an assurance that during your hard time this will help you and your family well-fed.

- **Helps to preserve and tenderize meat easily**

Water bath canning technique is not used to preserve meat. Pressure canning is only the option to preserve meat. Canning meat makes it super tender, so if you find a good deal on meat cuts then don't forget to scan them.

- **Eco-friendly method**

Canning method saves your energy. You can also can your own foods from your garden instead of buying processed foods from the store. So it also reduces the use of tins and papers. You can also reuse the jar again and again during pressure canning.

What is the difference between the water bath and pressure canning?

Water bath canning:

Water bath canning is used for high acid foods canning purposes. High acid foods are those food having pH values lower than 4.6. High acid food contains pickles, apples, peaches, pears, marmalades, jellies, jam, spaghetti sauce, ketchup, tomatoes, salsa, applesauce, and fruit butter. Heat is transferred to the food through boiling water and it can only heat at boiling water temperature. Water bath canning is one of the fastest methods compare with pressure canning.

Pressure canning:

Pressure canning is used for low acid foods canning purposes. Low acid foods are those foods having pH value higher than 4.6. Low acid food contains corn, beans, carrot, most of the seafood, potatoes, dairy products, stews, stocks, poultry, meat, peas, carrots, and green beans. Pressure canning heating the jar food above the boiling point. It takes several more time compared to water bath canning.

Tips

There are some helpful tips given below which makes your pressure canning journey easy

1. Skip the sterilization process if the canning process is 10 minutes or longer

Before canning, we immerse the canning jar into boiling water for 10 minutes to sanitizing them properly. New research taken by the National Center for Home Food Preservation shows that if the canning process time is 10 minutes or longer than 10 minutes, the jar will automatically be sterilized during processing time. Always remember to wash your canning jar into soapy water to clean dust and residues properly.

2. Make yummy and delicious jams from frozen fruits

In the summer season, a large number of fresh summer fruits are available in the garden. You can just store the fruits into your freezer and canned them after a week. This will help to reduce the stress over excessive harvest. You can make a delicious blueberry jam from frozen fruits in any season.

3. Before sealing remove air bubbles from the jar

Bubbling is a necessary process to remove the air bubbles present in the jar. If there is an air bubble left in a jar after sealing, this will lead to the sealing process failure. You can use any long and thin utensil to remove air bubbles. Chopstick is one of the best options available in wood and plastic for the bubbling process.

4. Perfect and properly canned food lasts more than a year

Proper canning food is stored in a cool, dry, and dark place at the surrounding temperature in between 50°F to 70°F this will help to increase the shelf life of your canned foods. Proper sealing also maintains the color, texture, and flavour of food and it also depends on the quality of food you have used.

5. **Remove the jar bands after sealing**

Jar band is used during the processing to hold the lid at its place. After finishing the process allow the jar to cooled down when the jar is cooled, and the lid is sealed then remove these jar bands and store them for next use.

How to Choose the Suitable Pressure Canner?

There are lots of pressure canner manufacturers are available in the market wisely choose your pressure canner as per your family requirements. There are various things to consider when choosing the right pressure canner for you.

1. **Choose the right size pressure canner**

Pressure canners are available in the market into different sizes. As per your family members you have to choose the sizes if you are single or couples then you have to go with a small size. If your family members are more than five, then a large pressure canner is the best option for you. Small canners are portable and lightweight as compare with the large canner. Large canners are heavy and mostly used for commercial purposes.

2. **Choose the best pressure canner as per pricing**

Pressure canners are long-lasting products choose it as per your budget. If your budget is low, then go with Presto pressure canner. It is one of the economic pressure canners I have used for the last 13 years. If you want a long-life pressure canner and your budget is high, then you have chosen premier pressure canner such as All-American canner.

3. **Care and Maintenance**

There are two types of pressure canners one is dial gauge and the other is weighted gauge. The dial gauge pressure canner requires once a year check into your local extension office for correct PSI (Per square inch of pressure). On the other side, a weighted pressure canner doesn't require such a check. You need to check the gasket regularly for any damage.

4. **Body materials used**

Pressure canners are available in the market into two different variants of body materials one comes with aluminium and the other is stainless steel both have their own advantages and disadvantages. The aluminium variant is portable and lightweight compare to stainless steel variants, but stainless steel is long-lasting as compared to aluminium.

FAQs

How long we have store canned food?

A properly canned food can long last at least one year if it is stored in dry, cool, and dark place with surrounding temperature maintains between 50°F to 70°F the cooler temperature is better. The surrounding temperature decides how long your food is safe for eating.

Why should I use pressure canning?

Pressure canning is used to increase the shelf life of your food for more than one year. It applies high pressure to your food and boils your food above the boiling point, this will kill the microorganisms from the food. Most of the food like fruits, vegetables, meat, sauces, and stew are low in acid. Low acid food means whose pH value is more than 4.6 and these foods are processed under higher heat into pressure canning.

When requiring jar sterilization?

The jar is immersed in a hot water bath for sterilization only when the processing time is less than 10 minutes. If the processing time is 10 minutes or more then 10 minutes there is no need for sterilization of jar.

Is headspace being important in pressure canning?

Yes, proper headspace is very important during processing. If the headspace is very less, then there are chances to expand food and air bubbles being forced the lid for leakage. If the headspace is too much, then jar may not seal properly, and the upper layer of food gets discolor.

Is it possible to reseal jar if the lid does not seal properly?

Yes, you can reseal the jar but make sure resealed within 24 hours only. For resealing you just replace the lid with another and reprocess the jar by applying the same pressure and time which applies before resealing.

Chapter 2: Canned Fruits Recipes

Canned Pears

Preparation Time: 10 minutes
Cooking Time: 25 minutes
Serve: 7

Ingredients:

- 18 lbs pears, peel & slice
- 6 cups water
- 1 cup sugar

Directions:

1. Add water and sugar in a saucepan and bring to boil over medium heat.
2. Once sugar syrup begins to boil then reduce heat to low.
3. Add pears and into the sugar syrup and simmer for 5 minutes.
4. Pack pears into the clean jars. Leave ¼-inch headspace.
5. Pour hot sugar syrup over pears. Leave ¼-inch headspace. Remove air bubbles.
6. Seal jars with lids and process in a boiling water bath for 20 minutes.
7. Remove jars from the water bath and let it cool completely.
8. Check seals of jars. Label and store.

Nutritional Value (Amount per Serving):

- Calories 784
- Fat 1.7 g
- Carbohydrates 206.5 g
- Sugar 142.5 g
- Protein 4.3 g
- Cholesterol 0 mg

Canned Oranges

Preparation Time: 10 minutes
Cooking Time: 15 minutes
Serve: 6

Ingredients:

- 3 oranges, peel, remove white pith & divide into segments
- 5 whole cloves
- 2 cups water
- ½ tsp cinnamon
- 1 cup sugar

Directions:

1. Add sugar and water in a saucepan. Stir in cinnamon. Bring to boil.
2. Reduce heat and simmer for 5 minutes.
3. Pack orange segments into the clean jars and top with cloves.
4. Pour hot sugar syrup over orange. Leave ¼-inch headspace. Remove air bubbles.
5. Seal jars with lids and process in a boiling water bath for 10 minutes.
6. Remove jars from the water bath and let it cool completely.
7. Check seals of jars. Label and store.

Nutritional Value (Amount per Serving):

- Calories 169
- Fat 0.1 g
- Carbohydrates 44.3 g
- Sugar 41.9 g
- Protein 0.9 g
- Cholesterol 0 mg

Canned Blueberries

Preparation Time: 10 minutes
Cooking Time: 20 minutes
Serve: 4

Ingredients:

- 3 lbs blueberries, rinse
- 4 cups Water
- 1 cup sugar

Directions:

1. Add water and sugar in a saucepan and bring to boil, stir until sugar is dissolved.
2. Pack blueberries in clean jars then pour hot sugar syrup over blueberries. Leave 1/2-inch headspace.
3. Seal jars with lids and process in a boiling water bath for 20 minutes.
4. Remove jars from the water bath and let it cool completely.
5. Check seals of jars. Label and store.

Nutritional Value (Amount per Serving):

- Calories 382
- Fat 1.2 g
- Carbohydrates 99.3 g
- Sugar 83.8 g
- Protein 2.6 g
- Cholesterol 0 mg

Canned Pineapple

Preparation Time: 10 minutes
Cooking Time: 60 minutes
Serve: 24

Ingredients:

- 6 large pineapples, peeled, cored & cut into chunks
- 5 cups water
- 1 cup sugar

Directions:

1. Add sugar and water into the pot and bring to boil, stir constantly until sugar is dissolved. Reduce heat to low.
2. Add pineapples chunks and cook for 10 minutes.
3. Pack pineapple chunks into the clean jars. Leave ½-inch headspace.
4. Pour hot sugar syrup over pineapple chunks. Leave ½-inch headspace. Remove air bubbles.
5. Seal jars with lids and process in a boiling water bath for 10 minutes.
6. Remove jars from the water bath and let it cool completely.
7. Check seals of jars. Label and store.

Nutritional Value (Amount per Serving):

- Calories 72
- Fat 0.1 g
- Carbohydrates 19.2 g
- Sugar 16.5 g
- Protein 0.4 g
- Cholesterol 0 mg

Canned Cherries

Preparation Time: 10 minutes
Cooking Time: 15 minutes
Serve: 4

Ingredients:

- 2 cups cherries, pitted
- 4 whole allspice
- 1 small cinnamon stick
- 1 tsp vanilla extract
- 1 tbsp lemon juice
- 1 cup water
- 1 cup sugar

Directions:

1. Add water and sugar in a saucepan and bring to boil, stir until sugar is dissolved.
2. Remove saucepan from heat and let cool.
3. Add vanilla extract and lemon juice and stir well.
4. Add allspice and cinnamon into each jar then add cherries. Leave 3/4-inch headspace.
5. Pour sugar syrup over cherries. Leave ½-inch headspace.
6. Seal jar with lid and store in the refrigerator.

Nutritional Value (Amount per Serving):

- Calories 230
- Fat 0.3 g
- Carbohydrates 59.7 g
- Sugar 56.7 g
- Protein 0.8 g
- Cholesterol 0 mg

Canned Apricots

Preparation Time: 10 minutes
Cooking Time: 20 minutes
Serve: 8

Ingredients:

- 2 lbs apricots, wash, cut in half and remove the stone
- 4 cups water
- 2 cups sugar

Directions:

1. Add water and sugar in a pot and cook over medium heat until sugar is melted.
2. Add apricots into the jars.
3. Pour sugar syrup over apricots.
4. Cover jars with lids.
5. Place jars in a large pot and cover them with water. Bring to the boil and simmer for 30 minutes.
6. Turn off the heat and let the jars cool completely.
7. Check seals of jars. Label and store.

Nutritional Value (Amount per Serving):

- Calories 240
- Fat 1 g
- Carbohydrates 62 g
- Sugar 60 g
- Protein 1.5 g
- Cholesterol 0 mg

Fermented Cranberries

Preparation Time: 10 minutes
Cooking Time: 10 minutes
Serve: 16

Ingredients:

- 3 cups fresh cranberries, slightly crush cranberry skins
- 2 cups honey
- 1 orange juice
- 1 cinnamon stick
- 1 tbsp ginger, sliced

Directions:

1. Add cranberries, orange juice, cinnamon stick, and ginger into the jars.
2. Pour enough honey to cover cranberries.
3. Seal the jar with a lid and shake jar 2-3 times to coat cranberries in the honey.
4. Loosen the jar lid and place jar in a dark place to ferment.
5. Every few days tighten the jar lid and give the jar a few shakes. Ferment at least a few weeks.

Nutritional Value (Amount per Serving):

- Calories 144
- Fat 0 g
- Carbohydrates 37.6 g
- Sugar 36 g
- Protein 0.2 g
- Cholesterol 0 mg

Canned Strawberries

Preparation Time: 10 minutes
Cooking Time: 20 minutes
Serve: 4

Ingredients:

- 4 cups strawberries, washed & hulled
- ¼ tsp citric acid
- ½ cup sugar

Directions:

1. Add strawberries and sugar in a large pot, cover, and let sit for 6 hours.
2. Add citric acid and place pot on heat and cook for 1 minute or until strawberries are heated through.
3. Remove pot from heat. Pack strawberries into the clean jars and cover with strawberry juice liquid. Leave 1/2 -inch headspace. Remove air bubbles.
4. Seal jars with lids and process in a boiling water bath for 10 minutes.
5. Remove jars from the water bath and let it cool completely.
6. Check seals of jars. Label and store.

Nutritional Value (Amount per Serving):

- Calories 140
- Fat 0.4 g
- Carbohydrates 36.1 g
- Sugar 32.1 g
- Protein 1 g
- Cholesterol 0 mg

Canned Peaches

Preparation Time: 10 minutes
Cooking Time: 30 minutes
Serve: 8

Ingredients:

- 4 lbs peaches
- 8 cups water
- 1 ½ cups sugar

Directions:

1. Add peaches into the boiling water and cook for 3 minutes.
2. Remove peaches from boiling water and place into the bowl of ice water.
3. Peel peaches discard the pit and cut into slices.
4. Pack peaches into the clean jars. Leave ¼-inch headspace.
5. Add water and sugar in a saucepan and bring to boil, stir until sugar is dissolved.
6. Pour hot sugar syrup over pears. Leave ¼-inch headspace. Remove air bubbles.
7. Seal jars with lids and process in a boiling water bath for 20 minutes.
8. Remove jars from the water bath and let it cool completely.
9. Check seals of jars. Label and store.

Nutritional Value (Amount per Serving):

- Calories 170
- Fat 0.2 g
- Carbohydrates 44.5 g
- Sugar 44.5 g
- Protein 0.7 g
- Cholesterol 0 mg

Canned Mango

Preparation Time: 10 minutes
Cooking Time: 30 minutes
Serve: 6

Ingredients:

- 8 mangoes, peeled, seeded & cut into chunks
- 4 tbsp sugar
- 3 tbsp fresh lemon juice
- Water

Directions:

1. Pack mango into the jars. Leave ½-inch headspace.
2. Add 1 tablespoon of lemon juice to each jar.
3. Add 2 cups of water and sugar in a pot and bring to boil. Stir until sugar is dissolved.
4. Pour hot sugar syrup over the mangoes.
5. Seal jar with lids. Process in a water bath canner for 15 minutes.
6. Remove jars from the water bath and let it cool completely.
7. Check seals of jars. Label and store.

Nutritional Value (Amount per Serving):

- Calories 300
- Fat 2 g
- Carbohydrates 75 g
- Sugar 70 g
- Protein 3 g
- Cholesterol 0 mg

Chapter 3: Canned Vegetable Recipes

Canned Green Beans

Preparation Time: 10 minutes
Cooking Time: 10 minutes
Serve: 14

Ingredients:

- 5 lbs green beans, washed and trimmed
- 14 garlic cloves, peeled and cut in half
- ¾ cup sugar
- 3 cups water
- 6 cups white vinegar
- 1 tbsp salt

Directions:

1. Add vinegar, sugar, water, and salt in a saucepan and bring to boil. Reduce heat and simmer for 3 minutes.
2. Add 2 garlic cloves to each jar. Pack green beans into the jar.
3. Pour hot brine over green beans. Leave ½-inch headspace. Remove air bubbles.
4. Seal jars with lids and process in a boiling water bath for 10 minutes.
5. Remove jars from the water bath and let it cool completely.
6. Check seals of jars. Label and store.

Nutritional Value (Amount per Serving):

- Calories 116
- Fat 0.2 g
- Carbohydrates 24.2 g
- Sugar 13.4 g
- Protein 3.1 g
- Cholesterol 0 mg

Canned Zucchini

Preparation Time: 10 minutes
Cooking Time: 10 minutes
Serve: 6

Ingredients:

- 3 lbs zucchini, cut into ¼-inch thick slices
- 5 black peppercorns
- 2 bay leaves
- 1 cup vinegar
- 1 cup sugar
- 8 cups water
- 1 red pepper, sliced
- 4 dill sprigs
- 12 baby carrots, cut into strips
- 3 garlic cloves
- 2 small onions, sliced
- 1 ½ lbs tomatoes
- 2 ½ tbsp salt

Directions:

1. Add water, vinegar, sugar, and salt into the large pot and bring to boil.
2. Evenly divide peppercorns, bay leaves, red pepper, dill sprigs, carrots, cloves, onions, tomatoes, and salt into the jars.
3. Pack zucchini into the jars. Remove air bubbles.
4. Seal jars with lids and process in a boiling water bath for 10 minutes.
5. Remove jars from the water bath and let it cool completely.
6. Check seals of jars. Label and store.

Nutritional Value (Amount per Serving):

- Calories 215
- Fat 0.8 g
- Carbohydrates 51.6 g
- Sugar 43.4 g
- Protein 4.4 g
- Cholesterol 0 mg

Canned Corn

Preparation Time: 10 minutes
Cooking Time: 30 minutes
Serve: 7

Ingredients:

- 4 ½ lbs corn kernels
- Water

Directions:

1. Pack corn in clean jars. Pour hot water over corn. Leave 1-inch headspace.
2. Add lids and rings. Place jar into the pressure canner.
3. Process can corn pints for 55 minutes, quarts for 85 minutes at 11 lbs pressure in a pressure canner.
4. Once done, cool canner, remove the lid and let jars stand for 10 minutes before removing from canner.
5. Remove corn jars from canner and place them on the counter for 2-3 hours.
6. Check seals of jars. Label and store.

Nutritional Value (Amount per Serving):

- Calories 85
- Fat 1.2 g
- Carbohydrates 18.6 g
- Sugar 3.2 g
- Protein 3.2 g
- Cholesterol 0 mg

Canned Squash

Preparation Time: 10 minutes
Cooking Time: 50 minutes
Serve: 12

Ingredients:

- 6 summer squash, cut into 1-inch cubes
- Water
- Salt

Directions:

1. Add squash and 6 cups of water into the pot and bring boil for 3-4 minutes.
2. Add squash into the clean jars. Leave 1-inch headspace. Add 1/4 teaspoon salt into each jar.
3. Pour boiling water over squash. Leave 1-inch headspace. Remove the air bubbles.
4. Add lids and rings.
5. Place jars into the power pressure cooker for 40 minutes.
6. Remove canned squash from the power pressure cooker and let it cool.
7. Check seals of jars. Label and store.

Nutritional Value (Amount per Serving):

- Calories 25
- Fat 0.4 g
- Carbohydrates 5.4 g
- Sugar 2.8 g
- Protein 2 g
- Cholesterol 0 mg

Canned Carrots

Preparation Time: 10 minutes
Cooking Time: 30 minutes
Serve: 14

Ingredients:

- 14 lbs carrots, wash, peel & sliced 1 ½-inch thick
- Water
- Salt

Directions:

1. Pack carrots into the clean jars. Leave 1-inch headspace.
2. Add 1 tsp salt into each quart jar.
3. Pour boiling water over carrots. Leave 1-inch headspace.
4. Add lids and rings. Place jar into the pressure canner.
5. Process can carrots: pints for 25 minutes, quarts for 30 minutes at 10 lbs pressure in a pressure canner.
6. Once done, cool canner, remove the lid and let jars stand for 10 minutes before removing from canner.
7. Remove carrots jars from canner and place them on the counter for 12 hours.
8. Check seals of jars. Label and store.

Nutritional Value (Amount per Serving):

- Calories 186
- Fat 0 g
- Carbohydrates 44.6 g
- Sugar 22.3 g
- Protein 3.7 g
- Cholesterol 0 mg

Canned Potatoes

Preparation Time: 10 minutes
Cooking Time: 35 minutes
Serve: 12

Ingredients:

- 6 lbs potatoes, clean & cut into 2-inch pieces
- Water

Directions:

1. Add potatoes into the pot and cover with water. Bring to boil, reduce heat, and cook for 10 minutes.
2. Drain potatoes well.
3. Pack potatoes in a clean jar. Pour hot water over potatoes. Leave 1-inch headspace.
4. Add lids and rings. Place jar into the pressure canner.
5. Process can potatoes: pints for 35 minutes, quarts for 40 minutes at 10 lbs pressure in a pressure canner.
6. Once done, cool canner, remove the lid and let jars stand for 10 minutes before removing from canner.
7. Remove potatoes jars from canner and place them on the counter for 1-2 hours.
8. Check seals of jars. Label and store.

Nutritional Value (Amount per Serving):

- Calories 156
- Fat 0.2 g
- Carbohydrates 35.6 g
- Sugar 2.6 g
- Protein 3.8 g
- Cholesterol 0 mg

Canned Sweet Potatoes

Preparation Time: 10 minutes
Cooking Time: 1 hour 30 minutes
Serve: 12

Ingredients:

- 6 lbs sweet potatoes, peel & diced into 1 1/2-inch piece
- 2 ¼ cups sugar
- 5 ¼ cups water

Directions:

1. Add water and sugar in a saucepan and bring to boil. Reduce heat and simmer until sugar is dissolved.
2. Pack sweet potatoes into the clean jars then pour hot sugar syrup over sweet potatoes. Leave 1-inch headspace.
3. Add lids and rings. Place jar into the pressure canner.
4. Process can sweet potatoes: quarts for 1 hour 30 minutes at 10 lbs pressure in a pressure canner.
5. Once done, cool canner, remove the lid and let jars stand for 10 minutes before removing from canner.
6. Remove sweet potato jars from canner and place them on the counter for 2-4 hours.
7. Check seals of jars. Label and store.

Nutritional Value (Amount per Serving):

- Calories 408
- Fat 0.4 g
- Carbohydrates 100.7 g
- Sugar 38.6 g
- Protein 3.5 g
- Cholesterol 0 mg

Canned Okra

Preparation Time: 10 minutes
Cooking Time: 6 minutes
Serve: 8

Ingredients:

- 8 cups okra, chopped
- 8 tbsp apple cider vinegar
- Water
- 1 ½ tbsp sea salt

Directions:

1. Add water, apple cider vinegar, and salt in a saucepan and bring to boil.
2. Add okra and cook for 6 minutes.
3. Remove pan from heat. Add okra into the clean jars then pour the hot liquid over okra. Leave ½-inch headspace.
4. Seal jar with lid and store in the refrigerator.

Nutritional Value (Amount per Serving):

- Calories 43
- Fat 0.2 g
- Carbohydrates 7.6 g
- Sugar 1.5 g
- Protein 1.9 g
- Cholesterol 0 mg

Canned Beets

Preparation Time: 10 minutes
Cooking Time: 1 hour 20 minutes
Serve: 6

Ingredients:

- 10 lbs beets, wash & trim stems
- Water

Directions:

1. Add beets and water in a stockpot. Boil beets until tender, about 30 minutes.
2. Once boiling done them rinse beets in cold water. Drain, cool, and peel.
3. Pack beets into clean jars. Leave 1-inch headspace.
4. Pour boiling water over beets. Leave 1-inch headspace. Remove the air bubbles.
5. Add lids and rings. Place jars into the pressure canner.
6. Process can beets: pints for 30 minutes, quarts for 35 minutes at 10 lbs pressure in a pressure canner.
7. Allow to cool canner, remove the lid, and let jars stand for 10 minutes before removing from canner.
8. Remove beet jars from canner and place it on the counter for 2-3 hours.
9. Check seals of jars. Label and store.

Nutritional Value (Amount per Serving):

- Calories 335
- Fat 1.5 g
- Carbohydrates 75 g
- Sugar 60 g
- Protein 12 g
- Cholesterol 0 mg

Canned Tomatoes

Preparation Time: 15 minutes
Cooking Time: 60 minutes
Serve: 8

Ingredients:

- 15 lbs fresh tomatoes, peeled
- Fresh lemon juice
- Salt

Directions:

1. Add tomatoes in a large pot and cover with water. Bring to boil.
2. Boil tomatoes for 5-7 minutes. Stir frequently.
3. Add 2 tablespoons of lemon juice and 1/2 teaspoon of salt to each jar.
4. Pack tomatoes in jars then pour the hot liquid over tomatoes. Leave 1/2-inch headspace.
5. Seal jars with lids and process in a boiling water bath for 40 minutes.
6. Remove jars from the water bath and let it cool completely.
7. Check seals of jars. Label and store.

Nutritional Value (Amount per Serving):

- Calories 135
- Fat 1.5 g
- Carbohydrates 29 g
- Sugar 20 g
- Protein 6.7 g
- Cholesterol 0 mg

Chapter 4: Jam & Jellies Recipes

Mixed Berry Jam

Preparation Time: 10 minutes
Cooking Time: 40 minutes
Serve: 12

Ingredients:

- 3 cups strawberries
- 2 1/2 cups blackberries
- 2 1/2 cups blueberries
- 1 tbsp fresh lemon juice
- 7 cups sugar
- 1.75 oz fruit pectin

Directions:

1. Add all berries in a saucepan and cook over medium-low heat until berries are softened. Mashed berries using a masher.
2. In a cup, mix together pectin, 2 cups of sugar and pectin and add into the berry mixture and boil over high heat.
3. Add remaining sugar and boil for 1 minute. Stir constantly.
4. Remove saucepan from heat.
5. Ladle jam into the jars. Leave 1/2-inch headspace.
6. Seal jars with lids. Process in a water bath canner for 10 minutes.
7. Remove jars from the water bath and let it cool completely.
8. Check seals of jars. Label and store.

Nutritional Value (Amount per Serving):

- Calories 479
- Fat 0.5 g
- Carbohydrates 125 g
- Sugar 122 g
- Protein 1 g
- Cholesterol 0 mg

Blueberry Chia Jam

Preparation Time: 10 minutes
Cooking Time: 18 minutes
Serve: 8

Ingredients:

- 3 cups blueberries
- 3 tbsp maple syrup
- 3 tbsp chia seeds

Directions:

1. Add blueberries and maple syrup into the saucepan and bring to boil over medium-low heat. Cover and cook for 3-5 minutes.
2. Using masher crush the berries until get desired consistency.
3. Stir in chia seeds and turn heat to low. Stir frequently and cook for 10-13 minutes or until jam thickens.
4. Remove pan from heat and let it cool completely.
5. Pour jam in a clean jar. Seal jar with lid and store in the refrigerator for up to 2 weeks.

Nutritional Value (Amount per Serving):

- Calories 64
- Fat 1.1 g
- Carbohydrates 13.5 g
- Sugar 9.9 g
- Protein 1 g
- Cholesterol 0 mg

Apricot Jam

Preparation Time: 10 minutes
Cooking Time: 40 minutes
Serve: 6

Ingredients:

- 2 lbs apricots, wash, cut in half & pitted
- 4 tbsp lemon juice
- 1 cup sugar
- 1/2 cup water

Directions:

1. Add apricots and water in a saucepan and simmer over medium-low heat for 10 minutes. Stir constantly.
2. Add lemon juice and sugar and stir well and simmer for 40 minutes or until apricots mixture thickens.
3. Remove saucepan from heat.
4. Ladle jam in clean and hot jars. Leave 1/4-inch headspace.
5. Seal jars with lids. Process in a water bath canner for 10 minutes.
6. Remove jars from the water bath and let it cool completely.
7. Check seals of jars. Label and store.

Nutritional Value (Amount per Serving):

- Calories 201
- Fat 1 g
- Carbohydrates 50 g
- Sugar 47 g
- Protein 2 g
- Cholesterol 0 mg

Strawberry Jam

Preparation Time: 10 minutes
Cooking Time: 30 minutes
Serve: 12

Ingredients:

- 10 cups strawberries, Clean & remove stems
- 1.75 oz pectin
- 4 cups sugar
- ¼ cup tequila
- 1 lime juice
- 1 tsp salt

Directions:

1. Add strawberries into the large pot and mash strawberries using a masher.
2. Add lime juice and salt and stir well.
3. Mix pectin with ¼ cup of sugar and sprinkle over berries. Bring to boil and stir constantly.
4. When it to a hard boil then add remaining sugar and boil for 1 minute more.
5. Remove pot from heat. Stir in tequila.
6. Ladle jam into the clean jar. Leave ½-inch headspace. Remove air bubbles.
7. Seal jars with lids and process in a boiling water bath for 10 minutes.
8. Remove jars from the water bath and let it cool completely.
9. Check seals of jars. Label and store.

Nutritional Value (Amount per Serving):

- Calories 302
- Fat 0.4 g
- Carbohydrates 76.2 g
- Sugar 72.6 g
- Protein 0.8 g
- Cholesterol 0 mg

Plum Jelly

Preparation Time: 10 minutes
Cooking Time: 50 minutes
Serve: 16

Ingredients:

- 5 lbs ripe plums, slice in half & discard pits
- 6 ½ cups sugar
- 1 tbsp butter, unsalted
- 1/75 oz pectin
- 1 ½ cups water

Directions:

1. Add plums and water in a large saucepan and bring to boil. Cover and simmer over medium heat for 10 minutes.
2. Strain the plum juice by straining through a mesh strainer. Allow to drain for 30 minutes. Discard plums.
3. You will get 5 ½ cups of plum juice.
4. Pour the juice into the pot. Add pectin and stir well and bring to boil.
5. Add sugar and boil jelly for 1 minute.
6. Remove pot from heat.
7. Ladle jelly into the clean jars. Leave ½-inch headspace. Remove air bubbles.
8. Seal jars with lids and process in a boiling water bath for 10 minutes.
9. Remove jars from the water bath and let it cool completely.
10. Check seals of jars. Label and store.

Nutritional Value (Amount per Serving):

- Calories 320
- Fat 0.8 g
- Carbohydrates 83.8 g
- Sugar 83.4 g
- Protein 0.2 g
- Cholesterol 2 mg

Grapefruit Jam

Preparation Time: 10 minutes
Cooking Time: 45 minutes
Serve: 14

Ingredients:

- 9 grapefruits, Peel and separate segments
- 3 1/2 cups sugar

Directions:

1. Add grapefruit segments into the blender and blend until smooth.
2. Add blended grapefruit mixture and sugar in a pot and simmer until sugar is dissolved.
3. Turn heat to high and bring to boil.
4. Cook grapefruit mixture until reaches a temp. 220 F.
5. Remove pot from heat.
6. Ladle jam in clean jars. Seal jars with lids.
7. Process in a water bath canner for 10 minutes.
8. Remove jars from the water bath and let it cool completely.
9. Check seals of jars. Label and store.

Nutritional Value (Amount per Serving):

- Calories 215
- Fat 0.2 g
- Carbohydrates 55 g
- Sugar 55 g
- Protein 0.5 g
- Cholesterol 0 mg

Orange Jam

Preparation Time: 10 minutes
Cooking Time: 40 minutes
Serve: 6

Ingredients:

- 5 cups orange puree
- 1 cinnamon sticks
- 1-star anise
- 1 whole clove
- 1 cup sugar

Directions:

1. Add orange puree, spices, and sugar into the saucepan and simmer over medium heat for 20-30 minutes or until jam is thickened.
2. Remove pan from heat.
3. Ladle jam into the clean jar. Leave ½-inch headspace. Remove air bubbles.
4. Seal jars with lids and process in a boiling water bath for 10 minutes.
5. Remove jars from the water bath and let it cool completely.
6. Check seals of jars. Label and store.

Nutritional Value (Amount per Serving):

- Calories 242
- Fat 0.8 g
- Carbohydrates 58.9 g
- Sugar 45 g
- Protein 2.8 g
- Cholesterol 3 mg

Peach Jam

Preparation Time: 10 minutes
Cooking Time: 30 minutes
Serve: 14

Ingredients:

- 4 lbs peaches, peel, pitted & chopped
- 2 tbsp lemon juice
- 1/2 tsp nutmeg
- 2 1/2 cups sugar

Directions:

1. Add peaches into the blender and blend until get the desired consistency.
2. Add peaches, nutmeg, sugar, and lemon juice into a saucepan and cook over medium heat. Stir to dissolve sugar.
3. Bring to boil and stir constantly until the jam is thickened.
4. Remove saucepan from heat and let stand for 10 minutes.
5. Pour jam in clean and warm jars. Seal jars with lids. Process in a water bath canner for 10 minutes.
6. Remove jars from the water bath and let it cool completely.
7. Check seals of jars. Label and store.

Nutritional Value (Amount per Serving):

- Calories 150
- Fat 0.3 g
- Carbohydrates 40 g
- Sugar 40 g
- Protein 0.5 g
- Cholesterol 0 mg

Pear Jam

Preparation Time: 10 minutes
Cooking Time: 30 minutes
Serve: 10

Ingredients:

- 5 pears, peeled, cored, and cut into chunks
- 1/2 cup brown sugar
- 1 tbsp ginger, grated
- 1 lemon juice

Directions:

1. Add pears, lemon juice, sugar, and ginger to the large saucepan and bring to boil over medium-high heat.
2. Reduce heat and cook the jam for 10-15 minutes or until thickened.
3. Ladle jam into the clean jars. Leave 1/4-inch headspace.
4. Seal jar with a lid. Process in a water bath canner for 10 minutes.
5. Remove jars from the water bath and let it cool completely.
6. Check seals of jars. Label and store.

Nutritional Value (Amount per Serving):

- Calories 90
- Fat 0.2 g
- Carbohydrates 23 g
- Sugar 17 g
- Protein 0.5 g
- Cholesterol 0 mg

Strawberry Chia Jam

Preparation Time: 10 minutes
Cooking Time: 35 minutes
Serve: 8

Ingredients:

- 2 lbs strawberries, hulled
- 1 ½ tbsp fresh lemon juice
- 2 tbsp chia seeds
- ¼ cup maple syrup

Directions:

1. Add strawberries and maple syrup into the saucepan and cook over medium heat. After 5 minutes mash the strawberries using a masher.
2. Add lemon juice and chia seeds and stir well. Turn heat to medium-low and cook for a few minutes, about 30 minutes or until jam is thickened.
3. Remove pan from heat and let it cool completely.
4. Pour jam in a clean jar. Seal jar with lid and store in the refrigerator.

Nutritional Value (Amount per Serving):

- Calories 71
- Fat 1 g
- Carbohydrates 15.8 g
- Sugar 11.5 g
- Protein 1.2 g
- Cholesterol 0 mg

Mango Jam

Preparation Time: 10 minutes
Cooking Time: 40 minutes
Serve: 8

Ingredients:

- 4 cups mango, peel & chopped
- 3 cups sugar
- 1/2 cup lemon juice

Directions:

1. Add all ingredients in a saucepan and bring to boil over medium-high heat. Stir frequently.
2. Boil the jam for 20 minutes or until thickens.
3. Once the jam is thickened then remove the saucepan from heat.
4. Ladle jam into the jars. Leave 1/4-inch headspace.
5. Seal jars with lids. Process in a water bath canner for 10 minutes.
6. Remove jars from the water bath and let it cool completely.
7. Check seals of jars. Label and store.

Nutritional Value (Amount per Serving):

- Calories 295
- Fat 0.4 g
- Carbohydrates 77.9 g
- Sugar 77 g
- Protein 0.7 g
- Cholesterol 0 mg

Black Raspberry Jam

Preparation Time: 10 minutes
Cooking Time: 25 minutes
Serve: 8

Ingredients:

- 1 lb black raspberries
- 1 3/4 cups granulated sugar
- 1 1/2 tbsp lemon juice

Directions:

1. Add berries, lemon juice, and sugar in a saucepan and cook over medium heat. Mash berries and stir occasionally.
2. Once berries release their juices then set heat to high and cook berries until thicken.
3. Cook over high heat for 10 minutes or until get gel consistency.
4. Once get gel consistency then remove the pan from heat.
5. Ladle jam in clean and hot jars. Leave 1/4-inch headspace.
6. Seal jars with lids. Process in a water bath canner for 10 minutes.
7. Remove jars from the water bath and let it cool completely.
8. Check seals of jars. Label and store.

Nutritional Value (Amount per Serving):

- Calories 205
- Fat 0.4 g
- Carbohydrates 50 g
- Sugar 46 g
- Protein 1 g
- Cholesterol 0 mg

Plum Jam

Preparation Time: 10 minutes
Cooking Time: 50 minutes
Serve: 12

Ingredients:

- 3 lbs plums, halved, pitted & quartered
- 3 cups sugar
- 1/2 cup lemon juice
- 1/2 cup water

Directions:

1. Add all ingredients in a saucepan and bring to boil. Stir until sugar is dissolved.
2. Stir for 15-20 minutes or until get gel consistency.
3. Remove pan from heat.
4. Ladle jam into the clean and hot jars.
5. Seal jars with lids. Process in a water bath canner for 10 minutes.
6. Remove jars from the water bath and let it cool completely.
7. Check seals of jars. Label and store.

Nutritional Value (Amount per Serving):

- Calories 180
- Fat 0.5 g
- Carbohydrates 47 g
- Sugar 47 g
- Protein 0.3 g
- Cholesterol 0 mg

Carrot Jam

Preparation Time: 10 minutes
Cooking Time: 15 minutes
Serve: 30

Ingredients:

- 1 1/2 lbs carrots, peel and grate 2 oz carrots
- 2 1/3 cup sugar
- 2 lemon juice

Directions:

1. Peel and chop remaining carrots.
2. Add carrots in the saucepan and pour enough water to cover carrots. Cook carrots until soften.
3. Drain carrots well and puree with a blender.
4. Add grated carrot, carrot puree, and sugar in a large saucepan and bring to boil for 5 minutes.
5. Remove saucepan from heat and let it cool for 10 minutes. Stir in lemon juice.
6. Pour jam into the clean jars and seal jars with lids. Label and store.

Nutritional Value (Amount per Serving):

- Calories 65
- Fat 0 g
- Carbohydrates 18 g
- Sugar 17 g
- Protein 0.2 g
- Cholesterol 0 mg

Chapter 5: Fruit Butter Recipes

Spiced Pear Butter

Preparation Time: 10 minutes
Cooking Time: 40 minutes
Serve: 8

Ingredients:

- 5 pears, peel & dice
- ¼ tsp nutmeg
- ½ tsp ginger, minced
- 1 tsp cinnamon
- 1 tbsp brown sugar
- 2 tbsp maple syrup
- 2 tsp lemon juice
- 1/8 tsp salt

Directions:

1. Add pears and remaining ingredients into the saucepan and bring to boil over medium-high heat.
2. Reduce heat to medium-low and simmer for 30 minutes.
3. Using immersion blender puree the pear mixture until smooth and simmer for 10 minutes more.
4. Remove pan from heat and let it cool completely.
5. Pour pear butter in a clean jar. Seal jar with lid and store in the refrigerator.

Nutritional Value (Amount per Serving):

- Calories 95
- Fat 0.2 g
- Carbohydrates 24.7 g
- Sugar 16.9 g
- Protein 0.5 g
- Cholesterol 0 mg

Mango Peach Butter

Preparation Time: 10 minutes
Cooking Time: 5 hours 30 minutes
Serve: 8

Ingredients:

- 3 lbs peaches, peeled & quartered
- ½ cup water
- 1 lemon juice
- 1 cup sugar

Directions:

1. Add all ingredients into the crockpot and cook on low for 2 ½ hours.
2. Stir everything well and cook for 2-3 hours more or until fruit mixture is softened.
3. Using immersion blender puree the fruit mixture until smooth.
4. Pour fruit butter in a clean jar. Seal jar with lid and store in the refrigerator.

Nutritional Value (Amount per Serving):

- Calories 116
- Fat 0.2 g
- Carbohydrates 30.3 g
- Sugar 30.3 g
- Protein 0.5 g
- Cholesterol 0 mg

Apple Pear Butter

Preparation Time: 10 minutes
Cooking Time: 1 hour 30 minutes
Serve: 6

Ingredients:

- 4 ripe pears, cored & diced
- 1 tsp vanilla
- ½ lemon juice
- ¼ tsp nutmeg
- 1 ½ tsp cinnamon
- 3 tbsp brown sugar
- ½ cup maple syrup
- 1 ½ cups apple cider vinegar
- 2 apples, peel, cored & diced
- Pinch of salt

Directions:

1. Add all ingredients into the blender and blend until smooth.
2. Pour blended puree into the saucepan and bring to boil over medium-high heat. Reduce heat and simmer for 30 minutes.
3. Stir well and continue to simmer for 1 ½ hour.
4. Remove pan from heat and let it cool completely.
5. Pour apple butter in a clean jar. Seal jar with lid and store in the refrigerator.

Nutritional Value (Amount per Serving):

- Calories 221
- Fat 0.4 g
- Carbohydrates 54.7 g
- Sugar 41.7 g
- Protein 0.7 g
- Cholesterol 0 mg

Cranberry Butter

Preparation Time: 10 minutes
Cooking Time: 4 hours
Serve: 4

Ingredients:

- 24 oz cranberries, rinsed
- 1 cup apple cider
- 1 cinnamon stick
- 1 cup brown sugar

Directions:

1. Add all ingredients into the crockpot and stir well.
2. Cover and cook on high for 2 hours.
3. Remove cinnamon stick and puree the cranberry mixture in the food processer.
4. Strain cranberry mixture through a mesh strainer.
5. Return cranberry puree into the crockpot and cook on high for 2 hours more.
6. Pour cranberry butter in a clean jar. Leave ½-inch headspace. Remove air bubbles.
7. Seal jars with lids and process in a boiling water bath for 10 minutes.
8. Remove jars from the water bath and let it cool completely.
9. Check seals of jars. Label and store.

Nutritional Value (Amount per Serving):

- Calories 260
- Fat 0.1 g
- Carbohydrates 58 g
- Sugar 48 g
- Protein 0.1 g
- Cholesterol 0 mg

Easy Apple Butter

Preparation Time: 10 minutes
Cooking Time: 8 hours
Serve: 10

Ingredients:

- 5 lbs apples, peel, core & diced
- 4 cups sugar

Directions:

1. Add apple and sugar into a crockpot.
2. Cover and cook on low for 8 hours.
3. Using blender puree the apple mixture until smooth. Leave ½-inch headspace. Remove air bubbles.
4. Seal jars with lids and process in a boiling water bath for 10 minutes.
5. Remove jars from the water bath and let it cool completely.
6. Check seals of jars. Label and store.

Nutritional Value (Amount per Serving):

- Calories 358
- Fat 0.2 g
- Carbohydrates 95.4 g
- Sugar 91.6 g
- Protein 0.3 g
- Cholesterol 0 mg

Peach Butter

Preparation Time: 10 minutes
Cooking Time: 45 minutes
Serve: 8

Ingredients:

- 4 lbs fresh peaches, peel & chopped
- 1/2 cup sugar
- 2 tbsp lemon juice
- 1/2 cup water

Directions:

1. Add peaches, sugar, and water in a saucepan and cook over medium heat until sugar is dissolved.
2. Turn heat to low and cook for 20 minutes or until peaches are tender. Stir frequently.
3. Remove pan from heat.
4. Add lemon juice and stir well.
5. Puree the peaches until smooth. Strain puree through a mesh strainer.
6. Return puree in a pan and cook over low heat until thickened, about 25 minutes.
7. Remove saucepan from heat. Ladle peach butter into the clean jars.
8. Seal jars with lids. Process in a water bath canner for 10 minutes.
9. Remove jars from the water bath and let it cool completely.
10. Check seals of jars. Label and store.

Nutritional Value (Amount per Serving):

- Calories 75
- Fat 0.3 g
- Carbohydrates 18 g
- Sugar 18 g
- Protein 0.5 g
- Cholesterol 0 mg

Cherry Butter

Preparation Time: 10 minutes
Cooking Time: 1 hour 20 minutes
Serve: 6

Ingredients:

- 2 lbs cherries, washed, pitted, & stems
- 1/2 cup brown sugar
- 1 cup sugar
- 1 tsp lemon juice
- 1 tsp vanilla

Directions:

1. Add cherries and sugar in a saucepan and cook over medium-high heat. Bring to a boil.
2. Reduce heat and simmer for 1 hour.
3. Remove pan from heat and add lemon juice and vanilla.
4. Puree the cherry mixture using a blender until smooth.
5. Return puree to the pan and bring to boil again.
6. Remove saucepan from heat.
7. Ladle cherry butter into the clean jars.
8. Seal jars with lids. Process in a water bath canner for 10 minutes.
9. Remove jars from the water bath and let it cool completely.
10. Check seals of jars. Label and store.

Nutritional Value (Amount per Serving):

- Calories 345
- Fat 0.2 g
- Carbohydrates 85 g
- Sugar 44 g
- Protein 0.5 g
- Cholesterol 0 mg

Apple Butter

Preparation Time: 10 minutes
Cooking Time: 40 minutes
Serve: 14

Ingredients:

- 10 lbs apples, cored and quartered
- 1 cup maple syrup
- 2 cups apple juice
- 1 tsp ground cloves
- 1 1/2 tsp ground allspice
- 1/2 tsp ground nutmeg
- 3 tsp ground cinnamon
- 1/2 cup water
- 3 tbsp lemon juice

Directions:

1. Add apples, water, and lemon juice in a saucepan.
2. Cover and simmer over medium-high heat.
3. Cook apples until softened, about 20 minutes.
4. Puree apple mixture until smooth.
5. Add pureed apple mixture into a slow cooker.
6. Add apple juice, maple syrup, and spices and stir well.
7. Turn slow cooker onto the high and cook until thick.
8. Ladle apple butter into the clean jars. Seal jars with lids. Process in a water bath canner for 15 minutes.
9. Remove jars from the water bath and let it cool completely.
10. Check seals of jars. Label and store.

Nutritional Value (Amount per Serving):

- Calories 160
- Fat 0.5 g
- Carbohydrates 41 g
- Sugar 30 g
- Protein 0.5 g
- Cholesterol 0 mg

Plum Butter

Preparation Time: 10 minutes
Cooking Time: 8 hours
Serve: 12

Ingredients:

- 8 cups plums, halved & remove pits
- 1 1/2 cups sugar
- 1/3 cup lemon juice

Directions:

1. Add plums, lemon juice, and sugar into the crockpot and cook on low for 8 hours.
2. Using blender puree the fruit mixture until smooth.
3. Ladle plum butter into the clean jars.
4. Seal jars with lids. Process in a water bath canner for 10 minutes.
5. Remove jars from the water bath and let it cool completely.
6. Check seals of jars. Label and store.

Nutritional Value (Amount per Serving):

- Calories 114
- Fat 0.3 g
- Carbohydrates 30 g
- Sugar 28 g
- Protein 0.5 g
- Cholesterol 0 mg

Blueberry Butter

Preparation Time: 10 minutes
Cooking Time: 6 hours
Serve: 16

Ingredients:

- 5 cups fresh blueberries
- 1 tsp ground cinnamon
- 1 lemon juice
- 1 cup sugar

Directions:

1. Add blueberries into the blender and blend until smooth.
2. Add blended blueberries and remaining ingredients into the crockpot and stir well.
3. Cover and cook on low for 1 hour.
4. Remove crockpot lid and cook on low for 4-5 hours until thickened. Stir frequently.
5. Ladle blueberry butter into the clean jars.
6. Seal jar with lid and store in a cool and dry place.

Nutritional Value (Amount per Serving):

- Calories 72
- Fat 0.3 g
- Carbohydrates 20 g
- Sugar 16 g
- Protein 0.5 g
- Cholesterol 0 mg

Cranberry Apple Butter

Preparation Time: 10 minutes
Cooking Time: 60 minutes
Serve: 12

Ingredients:

- 2 lbs fresh cranberries
- 2 lbs apples, cored and chopped
- 1 1/2 cups maple syrup
- 2 tbsp lemon juice
- 1 cup water

Directions:

1. Add apples, cranberries, water, and lemon juice in a pot and cover. Bring to a simmer over medium heat and cook until apples are softened.
2. Puree the fruit mixture until smooth.
3. Return puree to the pot.
4. Stir in the maple syrup and cook until the mixture is thickened.
5. Remove pot from heat and ladle apple cranberry butter into the clean jars.
6. Seal jars with lids. Process in a water bath canner for 20 minutes.
7. Remove jars from the water bath and let it cool completely.
8. Check seals of jars. Label and store.

Nutritional Value (Amount per Serving):

- Calories 165
- Fat 0.5 g
- Carbohydrates 38 g
- Sugar 30 g
- Protein 0.1 g
- Cholesterol 0 mg

Rhubarb Butter

Preparation Time: 10 minutes
Cooking Time: 50 minutes
Serve: 8

Ingredients:

- 1 1/2 lbs rhubarb, chopped
- 2 3/4 cups brown sugar
- 2 tsp vanilla
- 2 cups water
- 1 1/2 tsp cinnamon

Directions:

1. Add all ingredients into the saucepan and simmer over medium heat.
2. Reduce heat to low and simmer for 45 minutes.
3. Using blender puree the rhubarb mixture until smooth.
4. Ladle rhubarb butter into the clean jars.
5. Seal jars with lids. Process in a water bath canner for 10 minutes.
6. Remove jars from the water bath and let it cool completely.
7. Check seals of jars. Label and store.

Nutritional Value (Amount per Serving):

- Calories 214
- Fat 0.3 g
- Carbohydrates 53 g
- Sugar 50 g
- Protein 1 g
- Cholesterol 0 mg

Chapter 6: Marmalade Recipes

Lemon Honey Marmalade

Preparation Time: 10 minutes
Cooking Time: 40 minutes
Serve: 12

Ingredients:

- 8 cups lemons, chopped
- 6 oz liquid pectin
- 1 ½ cups water
- 4 cups sugar
- 2 cups honey

Directions:

1. Add lemons, sugar, water, and honey in a saucepan and bring to boil over medium heat.
2. Reduce heat and simmer for 30 minutes.
3. Add pectin and boil for 5 minutes. Stir constantly.
4. Remove pan from heat. Ladle the marmalade into the jars. Leave ½-inch headspace. Remove air bubbles.
5. Seal jars with lids and process in a boiling water bath for 10 minutes.
6. Remove jars from the water bath and let it cool completely.
7. Check seals of jars. Label and store.

Nutritional Value (Amount per Serving):

- Calories 468
- Fat 0.4 g
- Carbohydrates 127.5 g
- Sugar 116.6 g
- Protein 1.7 g
- Cholesterol 0 mg

Onion Marmalade

Preparation Time: 10 minutes
Cooking Time: 25 minutes
Serve: 4

Ingredients:

- 2 large onions, sliced
- 1 tbsp red wine vinegar
- 1/3 cup red wine
- 1 tsp sugar
- ¼ cup olive oil
- Pinch of salt

Directions:

1. Heat oil in a small saucepan over medium heat.
2. Add onion and cook for 10-15 minutes or until onion is softened.
3. Add sugar and cook for 5 minutes. Add wine and cook until wine is reduced.
4. Remove pan from heat. Add vinegar and salt and mix well.
5. Pour marmalade in a clean jar. Seal jar with lid and store in the refrigerator.

Nutritional Value (Amount per Serving):

- Calories 159
- Fat 12.7 g
- Carbohydrates 8.6 g
- Sugar 4.4 g
- Protein 0.8 g
- Cholesterol 0 mg

Blueberry Marmalade

Preparation Time: 10 minutes
Cooking Time: 45 minutes
Serve: 12

Ingredients:

- 4 cups blueberries, crushed
- 5 cups sugar
- 1/8 tsp baking soda
- 3/4 cup water
- 1 lemon, peel
- 1 orange, peel
- 6 oz liquid fruit pectin

Directions:

1. Chop lemon and orange rind and place in pan.
2. Chop lemon and orange pulp and set aside.
3. Add baking soda and 3/4 cup water to the pan and bring to boil. Reduce heat and simmer for 10 minutes. Stir frequently.
4. Add lemon and orange pulp, sugar, and blueberries. Return to boil.
5. Turn heat to low, and simmer for 5 minutes.
6. Remove pan from heat and let it cool for 5-10 minutes.
7. Add pectin and return to boil, stir constantly for 1 minute. Remove from heat.
8. Pour the marmalade into the clean jars. Leave 1/4-inch headspace.
9. Seal jars with lids. Process in a water bath canner for 10 minutes.
10. Remove jars from the water bath and let it cool completely.
11. Check seals of jars. Label and store.

Nutritional Value (Amount per Serving):

- Calories 352
- Fat 0.2 g
- Carbohydrates 92 g
- Sugar 90 g
- Protein 0.5 g
- Cholesterol 0 mg

Carrot Marmalade

Preparation Time: 10 minutes
Cooking Time: 40 minutes
Serve: 48

Ingredients:

- 2 cups grated carrots
- 2 ½ cups sugar
- 2 cups water
- 1 orange
- 1 lemon

Directions:

1. Shred orange and lemon in a large saucepan.
2. Add remaining ingredients into the saucepan and bring to boil over medium heat.
3. Reduce heat to low and simmer for 30 minutes or until thickened.
4. Once marmalade is thickened then remove the pan from heat.
5. Ladle the marmalade into the clean and hot jars. Leave ½-inch headspace. Remove air bubbles.
6. Seal jars with lids and process in a boiling water bath for 5 minutes.
7. Remove jars from the water bath and let it cool completely.
8. Check seals of jars. Label and store.

Nutritional Value (Amount per Serving):

- Calories 43
- Fat 0 g
- Carbohydrates 11.3 g
- Sugar 11 g
- Protein 0.1 g
- Cholesterol 0 mg

Strawberry Marmalade

Preparation Time: 10 minutes
Cooking Time: 20 minutes
Serve: 12

Ingredients:

- 4 cups strawberries, crushed
- 6 cups sugar
- 6 tbsp pectin
- 1 lemon

Directions:

1. Cut lemon peel and reserved lemon juice & pulp. Add lemon peel in a small pot with water and boil for 5 minutes. Drain lemon peels.
2. Add strawberries, sugar, pectin, lemon peel, lemon juice, and lemon pulp into the large stockpot. Stir well and bring to boil. Stir until sugar is dissolved.
3. Turn heat to high and boil for 1 minute. Stir constantly.
4. Remove pot from heat.
5. Ladle the marmalade into the clean and hot jars. Leave ½-inch headspace. Remove air bubbles.
6. Seal jars with lids and process in a boiling water bath for 10 minutes.
7. Remove jars from the water bath and let it cool completely.
8. Check seals of jars. Label and store.

Nutritional Value (Amount per Serving):

- Calories 396
- Fat 0.1 g
- Carbohydrates 104 g
- Sugar 102 g
- Protein 0.3 g
- Cholesterol 0 mg

Orange Marmalade

Preparation Time: 10 minutes
Cooking Time: 45 minutes
Serve: 6

Ingredients:

- 1 lb oranges, sliced thinly
- 1 tsp vanilla extract
- 1 cup sugar
- 1 cup water

Directions:

1. Add oranges and remaining ingredients into the saucepan and heat over medium heat. Bring to boil, reduce heat to low and simmer for 35-40 minutes.
2. Remove pan from heat and let it cool completely.
3. Pour marmalade in a clean jar. Seal jar with lid and store in the refrigerator.

Nutritional Value (Amount per Serving):

- Calories 163
- Fat 0.1 g
- Carbohydrates 42.3 g
- Sugar 40.5 g
- Protein 0.7 g
- Cholesterol 0 mg

Zucchini Marmalade

Preparation Time: 10 minutes
Cooking Time: 15 minutes
Serve: 12

Ingredients:

- 4 cups shredded zucchini
- 5 cups sugar
- 1 orange, peel, cut into segments and remove seeds

Directions:

1. Add orange segments and orange peel in the food processor and process until chopped.
2. Add zucchini, sugar, and orange in a saucepan and bring to boil over medium heat for 10-15 minutes or until thickened.
3. Remove pan from heat and let it cool completely.
4. Pour marmalade in a clean jar. Seal jar with lid and store in the refrigerator.

Nutritional Value (Amount per Serving):

- Calories 326
- Fat 0.1 g
- Carbohydrates 86.4 g
- Sugar 85.4 g
- Protein 0.6 g
- Cholesterol 0 mg

Pear Marmalade

Preparation Time: 10 minutes
Cooking Time: 10 minutes
Serve: 12

Ingredients:

- 4 medium ripe pears, peeled & quartered
- 5 ½ cups sugar
- 1.75 oz pectin
- 1 tbsp orange zest, grated
- 2 tbsp lemon juice
- ½ cup orange juice
- 8 oz crushed pineapple

Directions:

1. Add pears into the food processor and process until pureed.
2. Add pear puree, pectin, orange zest, lemon juice, orange juice, and pineapple into the saucepan and bring to boil over high heat. Stir constantly.
3. Add sugar and stir well and boil for 1 minute. Stir constantly.
4. Remove pot from heat and let it cool completely.
5. Pour marmalade in a clean jar. Seal jar with lid and store in the refrigerator.

Nutritional Value (Amount per Serving):

- Calories 393
- Fat 0.1 g
- Carbohydrates 104.1 g
- Sugar 99.8 g
- Protein 0.4 g
- Cholesterol 0 mg

Pineapple Marmalade

Preparation Time: 10 minutes
Cooking Time: 45 minutes
Serve: 18

Ingredients:

- 3 1/2 cups shredded pineapple flesh
- 1/2 lemon, sliced
- 4 1/2 cups sugar
- 4 cups water

Directions:

1. Add pineapple, lemon, and water in a saucepan. Cover and let sit for overnight.
2. Boil pineapple mixture for 20 minutes.
3. Add sugar and stir until sugar is dissolved.
4. Boil pineapple mixture for 25 minutes.
5. Remove saucepan from heat.
6. Pour the marmalade into the clean jars.
7. Seal jar with lids. Label and store in a cool and dry place.

Nutritional Value (Amount per Serving):

- Calories 202
- Fat 0 g
- Carbohydrates 53 g
- Sugar 53 g
- Protein 0.2 g
- Cholesterol 0 mg

Rhubarb Marmalade

Preparation Time: 10 minutes
Cooking Time: 35 minutes
Serve: 16

Ingredients:

- 6 cups fresh rhubarb, chopped
- 2 medium oranges
- 6 cups sugar

Directions:

1. Grind oranges into the food processor with a peel.
2. Add rhubarb, sugar, and grind oranges into the large saucepan and bring to boil. Reduce heat and simmer for 1 hour.
3. Remove pan from heat. Ladle the marmalade into the jars. Leave ¼-inch headspace.
4. Seal jars with lids and process in a boiling water bath for 10 minutes.
5. Remove jars from the water bath and let it cool completely.
6. Check seals of jars. Label and store.

Nutritional Value (Amount per Serving):

- Calories 302
- Fat 0.1 g
- Carbohydrates 79.8 g
- Sugar 77.7 g
- Protein 0.6 g
- Cholesterol 0 mg

Chapter 7: Pickle Recipes

Pickled Radishes

Preparation Time: 10 minutes
Cooking Time: 10 minutes
Serve: 6

Ingredients:

- ½ lb radishes, remove stem & root & cut into 1/8-inch slices
- 1 bay leaf
- ½ tsp ground black pepper
- 1 tsp mustard seeds
- ¼ cup water
- ½ cup sugar
- ½ cup apple cider vinegar
- 1 tsp salt

Directions:

1. Add sliced radishes into the clean jar.
2. Add vinegar, sugar, water, mustard seeds, black pepper, bay leaf, and salt into the saucepan and bring to boil.
3. Pour hot brine over sliced radishes.
4. Seal jar with lid and store in the refrigerator.

Nutritional Value (Amount per Serving):

- Calories 76
- Fat 0.2 g
- Carbohydrates 18.5 g
- Sugar 17.5 g
- Protein 0.4 g
- Cholesterol 0 mg

Pickled Sweet Peppers

Preparation Time: 10 minutes
Cooking Time: 5 minutes
Serve: 4

Ingredients:

- 2 cups sweet peppers, sliced
- 4 garlic cloves, minced
- 2 tbsp sugar
- ¾ cup water
- ¼ cup rice vinegar
- 2 tsp salt

Directions:

1. Place sliced sweet peppers into a clean jar.
2. Add vinegar, water, sugar, garlic, and salt into the small saucepan and cook until sugar is dissolved.
3. Pour hot brine over sliced sweet peppers.
4. Seal jar with lid and store in the refrigerator.

Nutritional Value (Amount per Serving):

- Calories 56
- Fat 0.2 g
- Carbohydrates 11.5 g
- Sugar 9 g
- Protein 0.8 g
- Cholesterol 0 mg

Pickled Carrots

Preparation Time: 10 minutes
Cooking Time: 10 minutes
Serve: 8

Ingredients:

- 1 lb carrots, peel and sliced into sticks
- 1 tbsp sugar
- 1/3 cup water
- 2/3 cup apple cider vinegar
- ½ tsp sea salt

Directions:

1. Pack sliced carrot sticks into the clean jar.
2. Add water, vinegar, sugar, and salt into the small saucepan and cook over medium heat until sugar is dissolved.
3. Pour hot brine over carrots in a jar.
4. Seal jar with lid and store in the refrigerator.

Nutritional Value (Amount per Serving):

- Calories 33
- Fat 0 g
- Carbohydrates 7.3 g
- Sugar 4.4 g
- Protein 0.5 g
- Cholesterol 0 mg

Pickled Beets

Preparation Time: 10 minutes
Cooking Time: 40 minutes
Serve: 12

Ingredients:

- 24 small beets, clean
- 1 cinnamon stick
- 2 cups sugar
- 3 1/2 cups vinegar
- Water
- Salt

Directions:

1. Add beets into the boiling water and cook until the beet is tender.
2. Drain beets well and peel and cut into chunks. Set aside.
3. Add 11/2 cups water, vinegar, cinnamon, sugar, and salt into the saucepan and bring to boil.
4. Reduce heat and simmer for 15 minutes. Discard cinnamon stick.
5. Pack beets into the clean and hot jars. Leave 1/4-inch headspace.
6. Pour hot water mixture over beets. Leave 1/4-inch headspace.
7. Seal jar with lids. Process in a water bath canner for 30 minutes.
8. Remove jars from the water bath and let it cool completely.
9. Check seals of jars. Label and store.

Nutritional Value (Amount per Serving):

- Calories 211
- Fat 0.5 g
- Carbohydrates 50 g
- Sugar 44 g
- Protein 2.5 g
- Cholesterol 0 mg

Pickled Peppers

Preparation Time: 10 minutes
Cooking Time: 10 minutes
Serve: 4

Ingredients:

- 1 lb banana peppers, seeded & sliced into the rings
- 1 1/3 cup sugar
- 4 cups vinegar
- 1 tsp celery seeds
- 1 tsp mustard seeds

Directions:

1. Add vinegar, celery seeds, mustard seeds, and sugar in a small saucepan and bring to boil over medium heat.
2. Add sliced banana peppers into the clean jars then pour hot brine over peppers.
3. Seal the jar with a lid.
4. Let it cool completely then store in the refrigerator.

Nutritional Value (Amount per Serving):

- Calories 315
- Fat 0.5 g
- Carbohydrates 70 g
- Sugar 70 g
- Protein 0.6 g
- Cholesterol 0 mg

Pickled Green Tomatoes

Preparation Time: 10 minutes
Cooking Time: 10 minutes
Serve: 6

Ingredients:

- 1 lb small green tomatoes, cut into small pieces
- 1 cup vinegar
- 8 cups water
- 2 garlic cloves, minced
- 2 tsp celery salt

Directions:

1. Pack tomatoes and garlic into the clean jars.
2. Add water, vinegar, and salt into the saucepan and bring to boil over medium heat.
3. Pour hot brine mixture over tomatoes.
4. Seal the jar with lids.
5. Let it cool completely then store in the refrigerator.

Nutritional Value (Amount per Serving):

- Calories 25
- Fat 0.3 g
- Carbohydrates 4 g
- Sugar 3 g
- Protein 1 g
- Cholesterol 0 mg

Pickled Cucumbers

Preparation Time: 10 minutes
Cooking Time: 60 minutes
Serve: 6

Ingredients:

- 1 cucumber, thinly sliced
- ½ cup water
- ½ cup apple cider vinegar
- 1 tbsp sugar
- 1 ½ tsp kosher salt

Directions:

1. In a medium bowl, mix together water, vinegar, sugar, and salt. Stir until sugar is dissolved.
2. Add sliced cucumbers into the bowl and let soak for 1 hour.
3. Pour pickled cucumbers into the clean jar and seal jar with a lid.
4. Once a jar is open then store in the refrigerator.

Nutritional Value (Amount per Serving):

- Calories 19
- Fat 0.1 g
- Carbohydrates 4 g
- Sugar 2.9 g
- Protein 0.3 g
- Cholesterol 0 mg

Pickled Jalapeno

Preparation Time: 10 minutes
Cooking Time: 15 minutes
Serve: 2

Ingredients:

- 10 jalapeno peppers, sliced into rings
- ½ tsp oregano
- 1 garlic clove, crushed
- 3 tbsp white sugar
- ¾ cup vinegar
- ¾ cup water
- 1 tbsp kosher salt

Directions:

1. Add water, oregano, garlic, sugar, vinegar, and salt into the saucepan and bring to boil over high heat.
2. Stir in jalapeno peppers. Remove pan from heat and let it cool for 10 minutes.
3. Pour pickled jalapeno with brine in a clean jar. Seal jar with lid and store in the refrigerator.

Nutritional Value (Amount per Serving):

- Calories 120
- Fat 1.1 g
- Carbohydrates 24.8 g
- Sugar 20.8 g
- Protein 1.2 g
- Cholesterol 0 mg

Pickled Brussels sprouts

Preparation Time: 10 minutes
Cooking Time: 20 minutes
Serve: 6

Ingredients:

- 3 lbs Brussels sprouts, cut stem ends then cut sprouts in half
- 15 black peppercorns
- 2 cups water
- 5 cups vinegar
- 6 dill heads
- 12 garlic cloves, smashed
- Salt

Directions:

1. Add water, vinegar, and salt in a saucepan and bring to boil.
2. Divide garlic, dill, and peppercorns evenly into the jars.
3. Pack Brussels sprouts into the jars tightly. Leave 1/2-inch headspace.
4. Pour hot water mixture over Brussels sprouts. Leave 1/2-inch headspace.
5. Seal jar with lids. Process in a water bath canner for 10 minutes.
6. Remove jars from the water bath and let it cool completely.
7. Check seals of jars. Label and store.

Nutritional Value (Amount per Serving):

- Calories 150
- Fat 1 g
- Carbohydrates 24 g
- Sugar 5 g
- Protein 8 g
- Cholesterol 0 mg

Pickled Cherry Tomatoes

Preparation Time: 10 minutes
Cooking Time: 10 minutes
Serve: 4

Ingredients:

- 4 cups cherry tomatoes
- 2 cups water
- 1 cup vinegar
- 2 sprigs fresh rosemary
- 2 garlic cloves
- 1/2 tsp salt

Directions:

1. Add vinegar, water, and salt in a saucepan and bring to boil over medium heat. Turn heat to low and simmer for 10 minutes.
2. Pack cherry tomatoes in clean jars.
3. Add garlic cloves and rosemary on top of tomatoes.
4. Pour hot brine over tomatoes. Leave 1/4-inch headspace.
5. Seal jar with lids. Process in a water bath canner for 10 minutes.
6. Remove jars from the water bath and let it cool completely.
7. Check seals of jars. Label and store.

Nutritional Value (Amount per Serving):

- Calories 45
- Fat 0.5 g
- Carbohydrates 8 g
- Sugar 5 g
- Protein 2 g
- Cholesterol 0 mg

Pickled Onions

Preparation Time: 10 minutes
Cooking Time: 10 minutes
Serve: 20

Ingredients:

- 1 red onion, thinly sliced
- 2 tsp sugar
- 1/2 cup hot water
- 2 garlic cloves, sliced
- 3/4 cup vinegar
- 1 tsp salt

Directions:

1. Pack sliced onion and garlic into the clean and hot jar.
2. In a bowl, whisk together hot water, sugar, vinegar, and salt until sugar is dissolved.
3. Pour water mixture over onions.
4. Seal jar with a lid.
5. Store in the refrigerator for up to 1 month.

Nutritional Value (Amount per Serving):

- Calories 6
- Fat 0 g
- Carbohydrates 1 g
- Sugar 0.5 g
- Protein 0.1 g
- Cholesterol 0 mg

Pickled Asparagus

Preparation Time: 10 minutes
Cooking Time: 10 minutes
Serve: 4

Ingredients:

- 1 lb fresh asparagus spears, trim ends
- 3 fresh dill sprigs
- 2 garlic cloves, peeled
- 1/2 tsp black peppercorns
- 1 1/2 tsp sugar
- 1 cup water
- 1 1/2 cups vinegar
- 2 tbsp salt

Directions:

1. Pack asparagus spears into the jars.
2. Add water, sugar, vinegar, and salt into a saucepan and bring to boil over medium heat.
3. Stir until sugar is dissolved.
4. Pour hot water mixture over asparagus. Leave 1/2-inch headspace.
5. Seal the jar with lids.
6. Let it cool completely then store in the refrigerator.

Nutritional Value (Amount per Serving):

- Calories 40
- Fat 0.1 g
- Carbohydrates 6 g
- Sugar 3 g
- Protein 2 g
- Cholesterol 0 mg

Chapter 8: Relish Recipes

Radish Relish

Preparation Time: 10 minutes
Cooking Time: 30 minutes
Serve: 32

Ingredients:

- 3 cups stemmed radishes
- 2 tbsp prepared horseradish
- 1 cup vinegar
- 1 tbsp mustard seeds
- 1 cup sugar
- 1 onion
- 2 celery ribs
- 2 tsp salt

Directions:

1. Chop radishes, onion, and celery finely and add into the large bowl. Add remaining ingredients and mix well and let sit for 3 hours.
2. Transfer vegetable mixture into the saucepan and bring to boil for 10 minutes.
3. Ladle vegetable mixture into the jars. Leave ½-inch headspace. Remove air bubbles.
4. Seal jars with lids and process in a boiling water bath for 20 minutes.
5. Remove jars from the water bath and let it cool completely.
6. Check seals of jars. Label and store.

Nutritional Value (Amount per Serving):

- Calories 30
- Fat 0.1 g
- Carbohydrates 7.2 g
- Sugar 6.7 g
- Protein 0.2 g
- Cholesterol 0 mg

Jalapeno Relish

Preparation Time: 10 minutes
Cooking Time: 45 minutes
Serve: 12

Ingredients:

- 2 lbs jalapenos, chopped
- 6 tsp sugar
- 1 ½ cups water
- 3 cups vinegar
- 2 tbsp oregano
- 4 garlic cloves, minced
- 1 onion, chopped
- 2 lbs tomatoes, chopped
- 6 tsp salt

Directions:

1. Add all ingredients into the large bowl and mix well and let sit for 10 minutes.
2. Ladle vegetable mixture into the jars. Leave ½-inch headspace. Remove air bubbles.
3. Seal jars with lids and process in a boiling water bath for 45 minutes.
4. Remove jars from the water bath and let it cool completely.
5. Check seals of jars. Label and store.

Nutritional Value (Amount per Serving):

- Calories 64
- Fat 0.7 g
- Carbohydrates 11.6 g
- Sugar 7.3 g
- Protein 1.9 g
- Cholesterol 0 mg

Cucumber Relish

Preparation Time: 10 minutes
Cooking Time: 30 minutes
Serve: 12

Ingredients:

- 4 cups ground cucumbers
- 1 tbsp mustard seeds
- 2 cups vinegar
- 3 ½ cups sugar
- 3 cups celery, diced
- 3 cups ground onions
- 1 tbsp celery seeds
- ½ cup ground red pepper
- 1 cup ground green pepper
- ¼ cup salt

Directions:

1. Add all vegetables into the large bowl. Add salt into the vegetables and mix well.
2. Cover vegetables with water and let sit for 4 hours.
3. After 4 hours drain vegetables through a colander.
4. Add vinegar, mustard seed, celery seed, and sugar in a saucepan and bring to boil. Stir until sugar is dissolved.
5. Stir in drained vegetables and simmer for 10 minutes.
6. Pack vegetables into the clean jars. Leave ½-inch headspace. Remove air bubbles.
7. Seal jars with lids and process in a boiling water bath for 10 minutes.
8. Remove jars from the water bath and let it cool completely.
9. Check seals of jars. Label and store.

Nutritional Value (Amount per Serving):

- Calories 266
- Fat 1.1 g
- Carbohydrates 66 g
- Sugar 61 g
- Protein 1.5 g
- Cholesterol 0 mg

Corn Relish

Preparation Time: 10 minutes
Cooking Time: 60 minutes
Serve: 16

Ingredients:

- 8 ears corn, husked & cleaned
- 1 tsp mustard seed
- 1 tsp celery seed
- 2 cups apple cider vinegar
- 1 cup sugar
- 1 cup onion, chopped
- ½ cucumber, chopped
- ¾ cup red bell pepper, chopped
- 1 ½ cups green bell peppers, chopped
- 2 lbs tomatoes, peel, seeded, & chopped
- 1 tbsp salt

Directions:

1. Cut corn from the cobs.
2. In a large saucepan, mix corn, onion, cucumbers, bell peppers, and tomatoes.
3. In a medium saucepan, mix sugar, vinegar, celery seed, mustard seed, and salt and pour over vegetable mixture. Bring to boil, simmer for 60 minutes.
4. Remove pan from heat.
5. Ladle relish in a clean jar. Seal jar with lid and store in the refrigerator.

Nutritional Value (Amount per Serving):

- Calories 141
- Fat 1.2 g
- Carbohydrates 31.9 g
- Sugar 17.9 g
- Protein 3.4 g
- Cholesterol 0 mg

Jalapeno Corn Relish

Preparation Time: 10 minutes
Cooking Time: 15 minutes
Serve: 16

Ingredients:

- 15 oz corn kernel, drained
- 2 garlic cloves, minced
- 1/2 bell pepper, diced
- 1/2 cup onion, diced
- 2 jalapenos, diced
- 1/2 tsp curry powder
- 1/4 cup brown sugar
- 1/2 cup vinegar
- 1/2 cup water
- 1/2 tsp sea salt

Directions:

1. In a large bowl, mix together corn, onion, jalapenos, garlic, and bell pepper and set aside.
2. Stir together the remaining ingredients in a saucepan and cook over low heat.
3. Stir until sugar is dissolved.
4. Pour saucepan mixture over corn mixture and mix well.
5. Pour corn relish into the clean jars.
6. Seal the jar with lids.
7. Let it cool completely then store in the refrigerator.

Nutritional Value (Amount per Serving):

- Calories 135
- Fat 2 g
- Carbohydrates 30 g
- Sugar 7 g
- Protein 5 g
- Cholesterol 0 mg

Onion Relish

Preparation Time: 10 minutes
Cooking Time: 35 minutes
Serve: 6

Ingredients:

- 8 cups onion, sliced
- 1 cup vinegar
- 1/4 tsp mustard seeds
- 1 1/2 cups sugar
- 1 tsp salt

Directions:

1. Add sliced onion to the boiling water and cook for 5 minutes. Drain well and set aside.
2. Add remaining ingredients to the saucepan and bring to boil.
3. Add onion to the saucepan and simmer for 5 minutes.
4. Pack onion to the clean jars. Leave 1/2-inch headspace.
5. Seal jar with lids. Process in a water bath canner for 10 minutes.
6. Remove jars from the water bath and let it cool completely.
7. Check seals of jars. Label and store.

Nutritional Value (Amount per Serving):

- Calories 255
- Fat 0.3 g
- Carbohydrates 65 g
- Sugar 55 g
- Protein 1.7 g
- Cholesterol 0 mg

Zucchini Relish

Preparation Time: 10 minutes
Cooking Time: 2 hours 35 minutes
Serve: 5

Ingredients:

- 4 medium zucchinis, chopped
- ½ tsp red pepper flakes
- 1 tsp coriander seeds
- 2 tsp ground turmeric
- 2 tsp mustard seeds
- 1 cup sugar
- 2 cups apple cider vinegar
- 3 tbsp kosher salt
- 1 orange bell pepper, chopped
- 1 red bell pepper, chopped
- 1 onion, chopped

Directions:

1. Add zucchini, peppers, and onion in a large bowl and toss with salt. Cover vegetables with water and let soak for 2 hours.
2. After 2 hours drain vegetables well and rinse.
3. In a large saucepan, add vinegar, turmeric, mustard seeds, sugar, red pepper flakes, and coriander and bring to boil.
4. Add drained vegetables, reduce heat and simmer for 10-12 minutes.
5. Remove pan from heat and let it cool completely.
6. Pour relish in a clean jar. Seal jar with lid and store in the refrigerator.

Nutritional Value (Amount per Serving):

- Calories 229
- Fat 0.9 g
- Carbohydrates 52.9 g
- Sugar 46.6 g
- Protein 3 g
- Cholesterol 0 mg

Zucchini Relish

Preparation Time: 10 minutes
Cooking Time: 50 minutes
Serve: 12

Ingredients:

- 10 cups zucchini, grated
- 3 cups vinegar
- 3 cups sugar
- 4 bell peppers, chopped
- 3 cups onions, grated
- 1 tsp celery seeds
- 1 tsp black pepper
- 1 tsp dry mustard
- 1 tsp turmeric
- Salt

Directions:

1. In a mixing bowl, mix together zucchini, onions, bell peppers, and salt. Cover and let sit for overnight.
2. Rinse the vegetable mixture with cold water in a colander.
3. Add vegetable mixture and remaining ingredients to the large saucepan and bring to boil.
4. Reduce heat to low and simmer for 30 minutes.
5. Ladle relish into the jars. Leave 1/4-inch headspace.
6. Seal jar with lids. Process in a water bath canner for 20 minutes.
7. Remove jars from the water bath and let it cool completely.
8. Check seals of jars. Label and store.

Nutritional Value (Amount per Serving):

- Calories 240
- Fat 0.5 g
- Carbohydrates 60 g
- Sugar 55 g
- Protein 2 g
- Cholesterol 0 mg

Jalapeno Pineapple Relish

Preparation Time: 10 minutes
Cooking Time: 40 minutes
Serve: 8

Ingredients:

- 8 cups pineapple, diced
- 4 jalapeno peppers, seeded & diced
- 1 cup vinegar
- 1 onion, diced
- 1 1/2 tsp ground coriander
- 1/2 cup sugar
- 1/2 cup water
- Salt

Directions:

1. Add jalapeno, pineapple, and onion into the food processor and process for 2-3 times to finely chop.
2. Add pineapple mixture into the large pot.
3. Add remaining ingredients and stir well and cook over medium heat. Bring to boil.
4. Reduce heat, and simmer for 25 minutes.
5. Ladle relish into the jars. Leave 1/2-inch headspace.
6. Seal jar with lids. Process in a water bath canner for 15 minutes.
7. Remove jars from the water bath and let it cool completely.
8. Check seals of jars. Label and store.

Nutritional Value (Amount per Serving):

- Calories 144
- Fat 0.4 g
- Carbohydrates 35 g
- Sugar 30 g
- Protein 1 g
- Cholesterol 0 mg

Green Tomato Relish

Preparation Time: 10 minutes
Cooking Time: 30 minutes
Serve: 10

Ingredients:

- 8 cups green tomatoes, sliced
- 1/2 tsp celery seeds
- 3 tbsp mustard seeds
- 2 cups sugar
- 2 cups vinegar
- 1 hot red pepper, chopped
- 2 sweet red peppers, chopped
- 3 cups onion, sliced
- 1/2 tsp turmeric
- Salt

Directions:

1. In a large bowl, add green tomatoes and salt. Cover and let sit for overnight.
2. In a large pot, mix together vinegar, onions, turmeric, celery seeds, mustard seeds, and sugar. Stir well and bring to boil and simmer for 5 minutes.
3. Drain tomatoes well. Add green tomatoes and peppers to the vinegar mixture and bring to boil. Simmer for 20 minutes.
4. Ladle relish into the clean jars.
5. Seal jar with lids and store in the refrigerator.

Nutritional Value (Amount per Serving):

- Calories 225
- Fat 1.5 g
- Carbohydrates 52 g
- Sugar 47 g
- Protein 3 g
- Cholesterol 0 mg

Chapter 9: Salsa Recipes

Mango Salsa

Preparation Time: 10 minutes
Cooking Time: 20 minutes
Serve: 6

Ingredients:

- 6 cups mangoes, chopped
- 2 garlic cloves, minced
- 1/2 tsp red pepper flakes
- 1 1/2 cups bell pepper, diced
- 1 onion, diced
- 1/2 cup water
- 1 1/4 cups vinegar
- 1 cup brown sugar
- 2 tsp ginger, grated

Directions:

1. Add all ingredients into the large saucepan and bring to boil over high heat.
2. Stir until sugar is dissolved. Reduce heat and simmer for 5 minutes.
3. Ladle salsa into the clean jars. Leave 1/2-inch headspace.
4. Seal jar with lids. Process in a water bath canner for 15 minutes.
5. Remove jars from the water bath and let it cool completely.
6. Check seals of jars. Label and store.

Nutritional Value (Amount per Serving):

- Calories 220
- Fat 1 g
- Carbohydrates 53 g
- Sugar 48 g
- Protein 2 g
- Cholesterol 0 mg

Green Tomato Salsa

Preparation Time: 10 minutes
Cooking Time: 55 minutes
Serve: 16

Ingredients:

- 5 lbs green tomatoes, chopped
- 2 tsp sugar
- ¼ tsp cayenne
- 2 tsp pepper
- 1 tbsp oregano
- ½ tbsp cumin
- ½ cup vinegar
- 1 cup lime juice
- 1 cup cilantro, chopped
- 5 garlic cloves, minced
- 4 red bell peppers, chopped
- 3 jalapeno peppers, chopped
- 6 onions, chopped
- 1 tbsp salt

Directions:

1. Add all ingredients into the large pot and mix well. Bring to boil, reduce heat and simmer for 30-40 minutes. Stir frequently.
2. Remove pot from heat. Ladle salsa into the clean and hot jars.
3. Seal jars with lids and process in a boiling water bath for 15 minutes.
4. Remove jars from the water bath and let it cool completely.
5. Check seals of jars. Label and store.

Nutritional Value (Amount per Serving):

- Calories 60
- Fat 0.5 g
- Carbohydrates 13.2 g
- Sugar 7.6 g
- Protein 2.2 g
- Cholesterol 0 mg

Peach Tomato Salsa

Preparation Time: 10 minutes
Cooking Time: 10 minutes
Serve: 16

Ingredients:

- 2 peaches, peel & chopped
- 1/8 tsp pepper
- 2 tsp brown sugar
- ½ tsp lime juice
- 2 tsp vinegar
- 4 oz green chilies, chopped
- 1 garlic clove, minced
- ½ tbsp dried cilantro
- ¼ onion, chopped
- 1 tomato, chopped
- ¼ tsp salt

Directions:

1. Add all ingredients into the large mixing bowl and mix well.
2. Ladle salsa in a clean jar. Seal jar with lid and store in the refrigerator.

Nutritional Value (Amount per Serving):

- Calories 34
- Fat 0.5 g
- Carbohydrates 7.5 g
- Sugar 5.2 g
- Protein 1 g
- Cholesterol 0 mg

Apple Salsa

Preparation Time: 10 minutes
Cooking Time: 30 minutes
Serve: 7

Ingredients:

- 5 apples, peeled, cored & chopped
- 3 lbs tomatoes, blanched & peeled
- 3 tsp ground cinnamon
- 2 1/4 cups vinegar
- 1 cup sugar
- 2 jalapeno peppers, chopped
- 2 cup green bell peppers, chopped
- 2 cups onions, chopped
- 1 1/2 tsp sea salt

Directions:

1. Add all ingredients into the large saucepan and mix well. Bring to boil and let it boil for 10 minutes.
2. Reduce heat and simmer for 1-2 hours or until apples are softened.
3. Using masher mash salsa until get desired consistency.
4. Ladle salsa into the clean jars. Seal jar with lids. Process in a water bath canner for 10 minutes.
5. Remove jars from the water bath and let it cool completely.
6. Check seals of jars. Label and store.

Nutritional Value (Amount per Serving):

- Calories 270
- Fat 1 g
- Carbohydrates 65 g
- Sugar 54 g
- Protein 3 g
- Cholesterol 0 mg

Sweet & Spicy Pear Salsa

Preparation Time: 10 minutes
Cooking Time: 1 hour 20 minutes
Serve: 14

Ingredients:

- 10 tomatoes, chopped
- 1 tsp red pepper flakes
- 1 tsp dry mustard
- 1 tsp oregano
- 2 tsp paprika
- ½ cup vinegar
- ½ cup sugar
- 4 garlic cloves, minced
- 3 red peppers, chopped
- 3 green peppers, chopped
- 2 cups onion, chopped
- 6 cups pear, peeled and chopped
- 1 tbsp salt

Directions:

1. Add all ingredients into the large stockpot. Bring to boil, reduce heat to medium-high, and cook for 20 minutes.
2. Reduce heat to medium-low and simmer for 60 minutes.
3. Remove pot from heat. Ladle salsa into the clean and hot jars.
4. Seal jar with lid and store in the refrigerator.

Nutritional Value (Amount per Serving):

- Calories 104
- Fat 0.5 g
- Carbohydrates 25.4 g
- Sugar 18.1 g
- Protein 1.8 g
- Cholesterol 0 mg

Tomatillo Salsa

Preparation Time: 10 minutes
Cooking Time: 50 minutes
Serve: 4

Ingredients:

- 2 lbs tomatillos, husked & cores removed, chopped
- 1/3 cup cilantro, minced
- 6 garlic cloves, minced
- 1 cup bell peppers, chopped
- 1 cup onion, chopped
- 1/4 cup lime juice
- 1/2 cup vinegar
- 1 tsp paprika
- 1 tbsp cumin
- 1/2 tsp salt

Directions:

1. Preheat the oven 260 C.
2. Spread tomatillos onto the baking sheet and roast for 20 minutes.
3. Remove tomatillos from oven and add into the food processor and process 2-3 times.
4. Transfer tomatillos into the large saucepan. Add remaining ingredients and bring to boil.
5. Reduce heat and simmer for 12 minutes.
6. Ladle salsa into the clean jars. Leave 1/2-inch headspace.
7. Seal jar with lids. Process in a water bath canner for 15 minutes.
8. Remove jars from the water bath and let it cool completely.
9. Check seals of jars. Label and store.

Nutritional Value (Amount per Serving):

- Calories 115
- Fat 3 g
- Carbohydrates 21 g
- Sugar 3 g
- Protein 4 g
- Cholesterol 0 mg

Cherry Salsa

Preparation Time: 10 minutes
Cooking Time: 30 minutes
Serve: 12

Ingredients:

- 4 lbs cherries, washed, stemmed, pitted & chopped
- 1 1/2 cups onion, diced
- 3 jalapeno peppers, chopped
- 1/4 cup cilantro, chopped
- 2 1/2 cups vinegar
- 1/4 cup lime juice
- 4 tsp garlic, chopped
- 2 tsp sea salt

Directions:

1. Add all ingredients into the saucepan and stir well. Bring to boil over high heat.
2. Reduce heat and simmer for 5 minutes. Remove pan from heat.
3. Ladle cherry salsa into the clean jars. Leave 1/2-inch headspace.
4. Seal jar with lids. Process in a water bath canner for 15 minutes.
5. Remove jars from the water bath and let it cool completely.
6. Check seals of jars. Label and store.

Nutritional Value (Amount per Serving):

- Calories 190
- Fat 0.5 g
- Carbohydrates 44 g
- Sugar 1 g
- Protein 1 g
- Cholesterol 0 mg

Corn Salsa

Preparation Time: 10 minutes
Cooking Time: 25 minutes
Serve: 6

Ingredients:

- 6 cups corn, cooked
- ½ cup vinegar
- 1 cup sugar
- 2 tsp ground cumin
- 2 tbsp fresh cilantro, chopped
- 2 garlic cloves, minced
- 1 cup onion, diced
- ¼ cup poblano pepper, diced
- 2 tsp jalapeno pepper, diced
- 2 lbs tomatoes, peeled, seeded, & chopped
- 2 tsp salt

Directions:

1. Add all ingredients into the saucepan and bring to boil for 15 minutes.
2. Remove pan from heat. Ladle salsa into the clean and hot jars.
3. Seal jars with lids and process in a boiling water bath for 25 minutes.
4. Remove jars from the water bath and let it cool completely.
5. Check seals of jars. Label and store.

Nutritional Value (Amount per Serving):

- Calories 295
- Fat 2 g
- Carbohydrates 70 g
- Sugar 45 g
- Protein 6 g
- Cholesterol 0 mg

Tomato Salsa

Preparation Time: 10 minutes
Cooking Time: 25 minutes
Serve: 12

Ingredients:

- 10 cups tomatoes, peel, cored and chopped
- 2 tbsp cilantro, chopped
- 3 garlic cloves, chopped
- 1 ¼ cups apple cider vinegar
- 2 ½ cups chili peppers, chopped
- 5 cups onions, chopped
- 5 cups green bell peppers, chopped
- 1 tbsp kosher salt

Directions:

1. Add all ingredients into the stockpot and bring to boil over medium-high heat. Reduce heat and simmer for 10 minutes.
2. Remove pot from heat. Ladle salsa into the clean and hot jars.
3. Seal jars with lids and process in a boiling water bath for 15 minutes.
4. Remove jars from the water bath and let it cool completely.
5. Check seals of jars. Label and store.

Nutritional Value (Amount per Serving):

- Calories 93
- Fat 0.9 g
- Carbohydrates 20 g
- Sugar 11.8 g
- Protein 3.2 g
- Cholesterol 0 mg

Mango Pineapple Salsa

Preparation Time: 10 minutes
Cooking Time: 30 minutes
Serve: 4

Ingredients:

- 2 mangoes, peeled and chopped
- 2 jalapenos, chopped
- 1 sweet pepper, chopped
- 1 onion, chopped
- 2 garlic cloves, minced
- 1 tsp ginger, grated
- 1/4 cup vinegar
- 1/4 cup lime juice
- 1/3 cup sugar
- 3 cups pineapple, chopped
- 1 1/2 lbs tomatoes, cored and chopped
- 1/2 tsp salt

Directions:

1. Add all ingredients into the large pot and bring to boil.
2. Reduce heat and simmer for 10 minutes. Stir frequently.
3. Remove pot from heat. Ladle salsa into the clean jars. Leave 1/2-inch headspace.
4. Seal jar with lids. Process in a water bath canner for 20 minutes.
5. Remove jars from the water bath and let it cool completely.
6. Check seals of jars. Label and store.

Nutritional Value (Amount per Serving):

- Calories 280
- Fat 1 g
- Carbohydrates 70 g
- Sugar 60 g
- Protein 4 g
- Cholesterol 0 mg

Peach Salsa

Preparation Time: 10 minutes
Cooking Time: 20 minutes
Serve: 8

Ingredients:

- 8 cups peaches, peeled, pitted & diced
- 2 cups onion, diced
- 2 cups chili peppers, diced
- 4 cups tomatoes, diced
- 1 cup lime juice
- 1 1/2 cups vinegar
- 6 garlic cloves, minced
- 1 tbsp sea salt

Directions:

1. Add all ingredients into the large saucepan and bring to boil over medium-low heat.
2. Reduce heat to low and simmer for 10 minutes. Stir frequently.
3. Ladle salsa into the clean jars.
4. Seal jar with lids. Process in a water bath canner for 15 minutes.
5. Remove jars from the water bath and let it cool completely.
6. Check seals of jars. Label and store.

Nutritional Value (Amount per Serving):

- Calories 116
- Fat 1 g
- Carbohydrates 25 g
- Sugar 20 g
- Protein 3 g
- Cholesterol 0 mg

Tomato Corn Salsa

Preparation Time: 10 minutes
Cooking Time: 25 minutes
Serve: 6

Ingredients:

- 5 lbs cherry tomatoes, chopped
- 1/2 cup lime juice
- 1 cup onion, chopped
- 2 cups corn kernels
- 1/2 cup cilantro, chopped
- 2 jalapeno pepper, minced
- 2 tsp salt

Directions:

1. Add all ingredients into the large saucepan and bring to boil.
2. Reduce heat and simmer for 10 minutes. Stir frequently.
3. Ladle salsa into the clean jars. Leave 1/2-inch headspace.
4. Seal jar with lids. Process in a water bath canner for 15 minutes.
5. Remove jars from the water bath and let it cool completely.
6. Check seals of jars. Label and store.

Nutritional Value (Amount per Serving):

- Calories 120
- Fat 2 g
- Carbohydrates 25 g
- Sugar 12 g
- Protein 5 g
- Cholesterol 0 mg

Chapter 10: Sauces Recipes

Chili Sauce

Preparation Time: 10 minutes
Cooking Time: 30 minutes
Serve: 12

Ingredients:

- 4 cups chili peppers, wash & chopped
- 1 tbsp ginger, grated
- 1/4 cup garlic, chopped
- 1 1/2 cups raisins
- 2 1/2 cups sugar
- 2 1/2 cups vinegar
- 2 tsp salt

Directions:

1. Add sugar and vinegar in a large saucepan. Bring to boil and stir until sugar is dissolved.
2. Add remaining ingredients and stir well. Bring to boil, reduce heat, and simmer for 5 minutes.
3. Remove pan from heat.
4. Puree the sauce using immersion blender.
5. Ladle sauce into the clean jars. Leave 1/2-inch headspace.
6. Seal jar with lids. Process in a water bath canner for 10 minutes.
7. Remove jars from the water bath and let it cool completely.
8. Check seals of jars. Label and store.

Nutritional Value (Amount per Serving):

- Calories 255
- Fat 1 g
- Carbohydrates 65 g
- Sugar 56 g
- Protein 2 g
- Cholesterol 0 mg

Blueberry Sauce

Preparation Time: 10 minutes
Cooking Time: 20 minutes
Serve: 6

Ingredients:

- 2 lbs blueberries
- 1 lb sugar
- 1 lemon juice
- 1 ½ tbsp cornstarch

Directions:

1. Add blueberries and sugar in a large bowl and mash berries using a masher. Cover and let sit for overnight.
2. Take 2 tablespoon blueberry juice. In a small bowl, whisk together blueberry juice and cornstarch and set aside.
3. Add blueberry and sugar mixture into the pan and bring it to boil. Add cornstarch mixture and cook over low heat for 10 minutes. Stir constantly.
4. Remove pan from heat.
5. Ladle sauce into the clean jar. Seal jar with lid and store in the refrigerator.

Nutritional Value (Amount per Serving):

- Calories 378
- Fat 0.5 g
- Carbohydrates 99 g
- Sugar 90 g
- Protein 1.2 g
- Cholesterol 0 mg

Spaghetti Sauce

Preparation Time: 10 minutes
Cooking Time: 5 hours 15 minutes
Serve: 18

Ingredients:

- 25 lbs tomatoes, peel and chopped
- 1 cup lemon juice
- 2 bay leaves
- 2 tsp Worcestershire sauce
- 2 tsp red pepper flakes
- 2 tsp dried basil
- 2 tsp dried parsley
- 4 tsp dried oregano
- 8 garlic cloves, minced
- 2/3 cup sugar
- ¼ cup canola oil
- 24 oz can tomato paste
- 4 onions, chopped
- 4 green peppers, chopped
- ¼ cup salt

Directions:

1. Add all ingredients into the large pot and bring to boil over medium-high heat.
2. Reduce heat and simmer for 4-5 hours.
3. Remove pot from heat and discard bay leaves.
4. Ladle sauce into the clean and hot jars. Leave ½-inch headspace.
5. Seal jars with lids and process in a boiling water bath for 15 minutes.
6. Remove jars from the water bath and let it cool completely.
7. Check seals of jars. Label and store.

Nutritional Value (Amount per Serving):

- Calories 191
- Fat 4 g
- Carbohydrates 36 g
- Sugar 26 g
- Protein 6 g
- Cholesterol 0 mg

Pear Sauce

Preparation Time: 10 minutes
Cooking Time: 30 minutes
Serve: 8

Ingredients:

- 8 pears, peel, cored and chopped
- ½ tsp vanilla extract
- ½ tsp ground ginger
- 1 tsp ground cinnamon
- 2 tsp lemon juice
- ¼ cup water

Directions:

1. Add all ingredients into the large saucepan and bring to boil. Reduce heat and simmer for 25-30 minutes.
2. Remove pan from heat and puree the sauce using a blender until smooth.
3. Pour sauce in a clean jar. Seal jar with lid and store in the refrigerator.

Nutritional Value (Amount per Serving):

- Calories 123
- Fat 0.3 g
- Carbohydrates 32 g
- Sugar 20 g
- Protein 0.8 g
- Cholesterol 0 mg

Cranberry Sauce

Preparation Time: 10 minutes
Cooking Time: 20 minutes
Serve: 4

Ingredients:

- 2 ½ cups cranberries, washed
- 2 cinnamon sticks
- 1 tbsp red wine vinegar
- ¼ cup water
- 1 cup sugar
- ½ cup wine

Directions:

1. Add vinegar, sugar, cinnamon sticks, and water in a large pot and bring to boil over high heat.
2. Once it begins to boil then add cranberries. Reduce heat to medium and boil for 5 minutes.
3. Remove pot from heat. Add wine and stir well. Discard cinnamon sticks.
4. Ladle sauce into the clean jar. Leave ½-inch headspace. Remove air bubbles.
5. Seal jars with lids and process in a boiling water bath for 15 minutes.
6. Remove jars from the water bath and let it cool completely.
7. Check seals of jars. Label and store.

Nutritional Value (Amount per Serving):

- Calories 226
- Fat 0 g
- Carbohydrates 56 g
- Sugar 52 g
- Protein 0 g
- Cholesterol 0 mg

Chipotle Sauce

Preparation Time: 10 minutes
Cooking Time: 1 hour 20 minutes
Serve: 6

Ingredients:

- 32 oz plain tomato sauce
- 1 cup honey
- 1 cup brown sugar
- 7 oz can chipotle peppers in adobo sauce
- 3 garlic cloves, minced
- 1/2 cup onion, chopped
- 1 tsp black pepper
- 2 tsp dry mustard
- 2 cups vinegar
- 12 oz can tomato paste
- 2 tbsp olive oil
- 1 tsp salt

Directions:

1. Heat oil in a saucepan over medium heat. Add onion and garlic and sauté for 2-3 minutes.
2. Add remaining ingredients and bring to boil, reduce heat to low, and cook for 15-20 minutes.
3. Puree the sauce using a blender. Cook sauce for 20-25 minutes more or until thickened.
4. Remove pan from heat. Ladle sauce into the clean jars. Leave 1/2-inch headspace.
5. Seal jar with lids. Process in a water bath canner for 20 minutes.
6. Remove jars from the water bath and let it cool completely.
7. Check seals of jars. Label and store.

Nutritional Value (Amount per Serving):

- Calories 335
- Fat 5 g
- Carbohydrates 75 g
- Sugar 70 g
- Protein 1 g
- Cholesterol 0 mg

Apple Sauce

Preparation Time: 10 minutes
Cooking Time: 1 hour 40 minutes
Serve: 6

Ingredients:

- 3 lbs hot peppers
- 2 apples, peel, cored and chopped
- 2 onions, chopped
- 1/2 tsp turmeric
- 1/3 cup mustard seeds
- 3 tbsp garlic, minced
- 2 cups vinegar
- 2 tbsp salt

Directions:

1. Add all ingredients into the saucepan and bring to boil.
2. Reduce heat to medium-low and simmer for 60 minutes.
3. Remove pan from heat and puree the sauce using immersion blender.
4. Ladle sauce into the clean jars. Leave 1/2-inch headspace.
5. Seal jar with lids. Process in a water bath canner for 15 minutes.
6. Remove jars from the water bath and let it cool completely.
7. Check seals of jars. Label and store.

Nutritional Value (Amount per Serving):

- Calories 180
- Fat 3 g
- Carbohydrates 33 g
- Sugar 20 g
- Protein 6 g
- Cholesterol 0 mg

Strawberry Sauce

Preparation Time: 10 minutes
Cooking Time: 20 minutes
Serve: 14

Ingredients:

- 2 lbs strawberries, sliced
- 1 cup sugar
- 2 tsp water
- ½ tsp pectin

Directions:

1. Add strawberries into the large pot and mash using the masher.
2. Reserved 4 tablespoons of strawberry juice.
3. In a small bowl, whisk together 4 tablespoons of strawberry juice and pectin and set aside.
4. Add sugar and water into the strawberries and bring to boil over high heat.
5. Slowly add pectin mixture and stir constantly for 2 minutes over high heat.
6. Remove pot from heat.
7. Ladle sauce into the clean jar. Leave ½-inch headspace. Remove air bubbles.
8. Seal jars with lids and process in a boiling water bath for 10 minutes.
9. Remove jars from the water bath and let it cool completely.
10. Check seals of jars. Label and store.

Nutritional Value (Amount per Serving):

- Calories 75
- Fat 0.2 g
- Carbohydrates 19.3 g
- Sugar 17.5 g
- Protein 0.4 g
- Cholesterol 0 mg

Marinara Sauce

Preparation Time: 10 minutes
Cooking Time: 2 hours 40 minutes
Serve: 10

Ingredients:

- 28 oz can crush tomatoes
- 28 oz can whole tomatoes
- 1 cup red wine
- 3 tbsp olive oil
- 5 garlic cloves, chopped
- 1 tbsp rosemary
- 2 sprigs thyme
- 2 sprigs basil

Directions:

1. Add oil into the stockpot and heat over medium heat.
2. Add garlic and sauté for 1 minute.
3. Add crushed tomatoes, whole tomatoes, and remaining ingredients. Stir well and break whole tomatoes.
4. Add wine and bring to boil. Reduce heat to low and simmer for 1-2 hours.
5. Remove pot from heat. Ladle sauce into the clean jars.
6. Seal jar with lids. Process in a water bath canner for 40 minutes.
7. Remove jars from the water bath and let it cool completely.
8. Check seals of jars. Label and store.

Nutritional Value (Amount per Serving):

- Calories 170
- Fat 5 g
- Carbohydrates 26 g
- Sugar 2 g
- Protein 5 g
- Cholesterol 0 mg

Pasta Sauce

Preparation Time: 10 minutes
Cooking Time: 60 minutes
Serve: 4

Ingredients:

- 40 tomatoes, blanched, peel, deseed
- 3 tbsp garlic, minced
- 2 onions, chopped
- 1 tbsp olive oil
- 2 tbsp fresh basil
- 2 tbsp fresh oregano
- Salt

Directions:

1. Heat oil in a large saucepan over medium heat. Add onion to the pot and sauté until onion is translucent.
2. Add garlic and fresh herbs and sauté for 30 seconds.
3. Add tomatoes and cook for 5 minutes.
4. Remove pan from heat. Puree the sauce mixture using immersion blender.
5. Return pan on heat and simmer sauce for 20 minutes.
6. Ladle sauce into the clean and hot jars.
7. Seal jar with lids. Process in a water bath canner for 40 minutes.
8. Remove jars from the water bath and let it cool completely.
9. Check seals of jars. Label and store.

Nutritional Value (Amount per Serving):

- Calories 261
- Fat 3 g
- Carbohydrates 54 g
- Sugar 35 g
- Protein 12 g
- Cholesterol 0 mg

Chapter 11: Chutney Recipes

Sweet & Spicy Apricot Chutney

Preparation Time: 10 minutes
Cooking Time: 20 minutes
Serve: 8

Ingredients:

- 6 oz dried apricots, chopped
- 1/3 cup raisins
- ½ tsp red pepper flakes
- 2 tbsp brown sugar
- 1 tbsp apple cider vinegar
- ½ cup pineapple juice
- 1 tsp fresh ginger, grated
- 1 garlic clove, crushed
- 1 onion, chopped
- 1 tsp olive oil

Directions:

1. Heat oil in a small pan over medium heat.
2. Add garlic and onion and sauté for 5 minutes or until softened.
3. Stir in the vinegar, pineapple juice, ginger, raisins, and apricots and cook for 10-15 minutes or until most of the liquid is absorbed.
4. Add sugar and stir well and cook for 2 minutes.
5. Remove pan from heat and let it cool completely.
6. Pour chutney in a clean jar. Seal jar with lid and store in the refrigerator.

Nutritional Value (Amount per Serving):

- Calories 58
- Fat 0.8 g
- Carbohydrates 13 g
- Sugar 9.9 g
- Protein 0.7 g
- Cholesterol 0 mg

Apple Chutney

Preparation Time: 10 minutes
Cooking Time: 15 minutes
Serve: 15

Ingredients:

- 6 medium apples, peel & dice
- 1 tsp red chili powder
- 1 cinnamon stick
- 2 tbsp sugar
- Salt

Directions:

1. Add apples into the pan and cook over medium-low heat.
2. Add sugar and cook until apples are caramelized.
3. Add cinnamon stick, chili powder, and salt and mix everything well and cook for 10-15 minutes.
4. Remove pan from heat and let it cool completely.
5. Using blender blend chutney until get desired consistency.
6. Pour chutney in a clean jar. Seal jar with lid and store in the refrigerator.

Nutritional Value (Amount per Serving):

- Calories 53
- Fat 0.2 g
- Carbohydrates 14 g
- Sugar 10.9 g
- Protein 0.3 g
- Cholesterol 0 mg

Perfect Apple Chutney

Preparation Time: 10 minutes
Cooking Time: 20 minutes
Serve: 4

Ingredients:

- 2 cups apples, peeled and chopped
- 2 tbsp fresh lemon juice
- ¼ tsp ground cinnamon
- ½ tsp ground cardamom
- ½ tsp cumin powder
- ½ tsp chili flakes
- ½ cup sugar
- ½ tsp salt

Directions:

1. Add apples and sugar in a pan and stir well and cook for 10-12 minutes over medium heat.
2. Add remaining ingredients and stir well and cook for 7-8 minutes or until chutney thickened.
3. Remove pan from heat and let it cool completely.
4. Pour chutney in a clean jar. Seal jar with lid and store in the refrigerator.

Nutritional Value (Amount per Serving):

- Calories 156
- Fat 0.3 g
- Carbohydrates 41 g
- Sugar 36.8 g
- Protein 0.5 g
- Cholesterol 0 mg

Cranberry Chutney

Preparation Time: 10 minutes
Cooking Time: 10 minutes
Serve: 4

Ingredients:

- 12 oz cranberries
- 1 tsp whole-grain mustard
- ½ cup brown sugar
- 1 orange juice
- ¼ cup vinegar
- 1 apple, peel & dice
- 1 tsp fresh ginger, grated
- ½ onion, minced
- 1 tbsp olive oil
- ½ tsp salt

Directions:

1. Heat oil in a pan over medium heat.
2. Add ginger, onion, and apple and sauté until onion is lightly brown.
3. Add remaining ingredients and cook for 10 minutes or until cranberries are pop.
4. Remove pan from heat and let it cool completely.
5. Pour chutney in a clean jar. Seal jar with lid and store in the refrigerator.

Nutritional Value (Amount per Serving):

- Calories 195
- Fat 3.7 g
- Carbohydrates 37.3 g
- Sugar 28.9 g
- Protein 0.5 g
- Cholesterol 0 mg

Mango Chutney

Preparation Time: 10 minutes
Cooking Time: 20 minutes
Serve: 4

Ingredients:

- 1 lb ripe mango, peel & dice
- ¾ cup brown sugar
- 2 whole dried chilies
- ½ cup vinegar
- 1 garlic clove, crushed
- 1 tsp ginger, grated
- ¾ cup water
- 2 cardamom pods
- 1 tsp coriander seeds
- 1 tsp cumin seeds
- 2 whole cloves
- 1 cinnamon stick
- 1 tsp salt

Directions:

1. Take a small piece of thin muslin cloth and tie up all the spices into a bundle.
2. Add mango, spice bundle, garlic, ginger, and water into the saucepan and cook for 10 minutes or until mango becomes mushy.
3. Add dried chilies, sugar, vinegar, and salt and stir well.
4. Turn heat to low and simmer for 15-20 minutes or until chutney is thickened.
5. Remove pan from heat and let it cool completely.
6. Discard spice bundle from the chutney. Strain chutney through a mesh strainer.
7. Pour chutney in a clean jar. Seal jar with lid and store in refrigerator up to 4 weeks.

Nutritional Value (Amount per Serving):

- Calories 182
- Fat 0.6 g
- Carbohydrates 44.7 g
- Sugar 42 g
- Protein 1.1 g
- Cholesterol 0 mg

Sweet & Spicy Peach Chutney

Preparation Time: 10 minutes
Cooking Time: 25 minutes
Serve: 8

Ingredients:

- 3 cups peaches, chopped
- 2 tbsp vinegar
- 4 black peppercorns
- 3 cloves
- 2 cardamom pods
- 1 bay leaf
- 1-star anise
- ½ tsp lemon zest
- 1 tbsp ginger, sliced
- 1 fresh red chili, chopped
- 1 cup sugar
- ¼ tsp salt

Directions:

1. Add all ingredients into the saucepan and cook over medium heat until the sugar has dissolved.
2. Boil chutney for 2 minutes. Using masher mash the peaches.
3. Once sugar is completely dissolved then reduce heat to medium-low and cook for 10 minutes or until thickened.
4. Remove pan from heat and let it cool completely.
5. Pour chutney in a clean jar. Seal jar with lid and store in the refrigerator.

Nutritional Value (Amount per Serving):

- Calories 119
- Fat 0.2 g
- Carbohydrates 30.8 g
- Sugar 30.3 g
- Protein 0.6 g
- Cholesterol 0 mg

Peach Chutney

Preparation Time: 10 minutes
Cooking Time: 12 minutes
Serve: 4

Ingredients:

- 1 ¼ cup peaches, peeled and diced
- 2 tbsp apple cider vinegar
- 1 tbsp brown sugar
- ¼ tsp ground cardamom
- ¼ tsp cinnamon
- ½ tbsp vegetable oil
- 1 garlic clove, diced
- 1 tsp ginger, diced
- ¼ onion, diced

Directions:

1. Heat oil in a saucepan over medium heat.
2. Add garlic, ginger, and onion and sauté until onion is softened.
3. Add vinegar, sugar, cardamom, and cinnamon and stir until sugar is dissolved.
4. Add peaches and mix well and cook for 5-10 minutes or until chutney is thickened.
5. Remove pan from heat and let it cool completely.
6. Pour chutney in a clean jar. Seal jar with lid and store in the refrigerator.

Nutritional Value (Amount per Serving):

- Calories 50
- Fat 1.9 g
- Carbohydrates 8.1 g
- Sugar 6.9 g
- Protein 0.6 g
- Cholesterol 0 mg

Green Tomato Chutney

Preparation Time: 10 minutes
Cooking Time: 1 hour 30 minutes
Serve: 12

Ingredients:

- 6 cups green tomatoes, chopped
- ½ tsp red chili flakes
- 2-star anise
- 1 cinnamon stick
- ½ tsp whole cloves
- 2 tsp fresh ground ginger
- 2 cups brown sugar
- 1 cup vinegar
- 1 small onion, chopped
- 1 tsp sea salt

Directions:

1. Add tomatoes, sugar, vinegar, and onion in a pot and cook over medium heat.
2. Add red chili flakes, star anise, cinnamon stick, cloves, and ginger and cook over low heat for 1 ½ hour, stirring occasionally to prevent from sticking.
3. Add salt and stir well and cook until chutney is thickened.
4. Remove pot from heat. Discard star anise, cloves, and cinnamon stick.
5. Pour chutney in a clean jar, leave ½-inch headspace. Remove air bubbles.
6. Seal jars with lids and process in a boiling water bath for 10 minutes.
7. Remove jars from the water bath and let it cool completely.
8. Check seals of jars. Label and store.

Nutritional Value (Amount per Serving):

- Calories 116
- Fat 0.2 g
- Carbohydrates 28.2 g
- Sugar 26.2 g
- Protein 0.9 g
- Cholesterol 0 mg

Tomato Chutney

Preparation Time: 10 minutes
Cooking Time: 2 hours
Serve: 48

Ingredients:

- 5 lbs tomatoes, chopped
- 3 cups green onions, sliced
- 5 red bell pepper, seeded & diced
- 2 tsp red pepper flakes
- 3 tbsp mustard seeds
- 3 ½ cups sugar
- 3 ¾ cups apple cider vinegar
- 2 ½ cups red wine vinegar
- 2 tsp ground black pepper
- 5 tsp sea salt

Directions:

1. Add red wine vinegar, apple cider vinegar, and spices into the large stockpot and bring to boil.
2. Add tomatoes, bell pepper, and green onion and simmer for 2 hours or until chutney reduced by half.
3. Once the chutney is thickened then remove the pot from heat.
4. Ladle chutney into the clean jars, leave ½-inch headspace. Remove air bubbles.
5. Seal jars with lids and process in a boiling water bath for 15 minutes.
6. Remove jars from the water bath and let it cool completely.
7. Check seals of jars. Label and store.

Nutritional Value (Amount per Serving):

- Calories 79
- Fat 0.3 g
- Carbohydrates 18.5 g
- Sugar 16.8 g
- Protein 0.9 g
- Cholesterol 0 mg

Sweet & Sour Cherry Chutney

Preparation Time: 10 minutes
Cooking Time: 30 minutes
Serve: 8

Ingredients:

- 1 ¼ lbs fresh cherries, pitted & chopped
- 1 tbsp olive oil
- 2 tbsp brown sugar
- 1 tbsp whole-grain mustard
- ½ cup red wine vinegar
- 1 tsp ginger, grated
- 1 garlic clove, minced
- 1/3 cup dried currants
- ½ small onion, diced
- 1 tsp kosher salt

Directions:

1. Heat oil in a pot over medium-low heat.
2. Add garlic and onions and sauté until softened.
3. Add vinegar and cook for 2-3 minutes.
4. Add cherries, mustard, sugar, ginger, currants, and salt and stir well. Simmer for 30 minutes, stirring frequently, until cooked and thicken.
5. Remove pot from heat and let it cool completely.
6. Pour chutney in a clean jar. Seal jar with lid and store in the refrigerator.

Nutritional Value (Amount per Serving):

- Calories 115
- Fat 1.9 g
- Carbohydrates 23.7 g
- Sugar 2.8 g
- Protein 0.4 g
- Cholesterol 0 mg

Chapter 12: Preserves Recipes

Preserved Fig

Preparation Time: 10 minutes
Cooking Time: 45 minutes
Serve: 14

Ingredients:

- 6 cups figs, trimmed & roughly cut
- 1 packet liquid pectin
- 1 tsp butter
- 1 tsp lime zest
- ¼ cup lime juice
- ½ cup water
- 7 cups sugar

Directions:

1. Add all ingredients except liquid pectin into the large pot and let sit for 30 minutes.
2. After 30 minutes place a pot on heat and bring to boil. Boil for 10 minutes.
3. Stir in liquid pectin. Stir constantly for 1 minute.
4. Remove pot from heat and let it cool slightly.
5. Ladle fig into the clean jars, leave ½-inch headspace. Remove air bubbles.
6. Seal jars with lids and process in a boiling water bath for 20 minutes.
7. Remove jars from the water bath and let it cool completely.
8. Check seals of jars. Label and store.

Nutritional Value (Amount per Serving):

- Calories 591
- Fat 1.1 g
- Carbohydrates 154.6 g
- Sugar 140.9 g
- Protein 2.8 g
- Cholesterol 1 mg

Preserved Lemons

Preparation Time: 10 minutes
Cooking Time: 15 minutes
Serve: 2

Ingredients:

- 2 lemons, rinse, score peel down length of lemons
- 2 tsp black peppercorns
- 2 tsp coriander seeds
- 1 cinnamon stick
- 1 bay leaf
- 3 whole cloves
- 3 cups water
- 2 tbsp kosher salt

Directions:

1. Add lemons, water, and salt in a saucepan and bring to boil. Reduce heat, cover, and simmer until the lemon peel can be pierced with a knife.
2. Transfer lemon to the clean canning jar. Reserved saltwater.
3. Add bay leaf, cloves, coriander seeds, cinnamon stick, and black peppercorns into the lemon jar.
4. Pour reserved saltwater over lemons, fill jar until the lemon is completely covered with saltwater.
5. Seal the jar with a lid and let it cool completely. Store in the refrigerator.

Nutritional Value (Amount per Serving):

- Calories 22
- Fat 0.2 g
- Carbohydrates 6.8 g
- Sugar 1.5 g
- Protein 0.9 g
- Cholesterol 0 mg

Blueberry Preserves

Preparation Time: 10 minutes
Cooking Time: 20 minutes
Serve: 6

Ingredients:

- 6 cups blueberries
- 2 lemon juice
- 3 tbsp pectin
- 2 cups sugar

Directions:

1. Add blueberries and lemon juice into the large pot and bring to boil. Stir frequently.
2. Mix ½ cup sugar and pectin and add it into the blueberries. Mix well return to boil.
3. Add remaining sugar and cook until thickens.
4. Remove pot from heat.
5. Ladle blueberries into the clean jars, leave ½-inch headspace. Remove air bubbles.
6. Seal jars with lids and process in a boiling water bath for 15 minutes.
7. Remove jars from the water bath and let it cool completely.
8. Check seals of jars. Label and store.

Nutritional Value (Amount per Serving):

- Calories 339
- Fat 0.5 g
- Carbohydrates 88.7 g
- Sugar 81.1 g
- Protein 1.1 g
- Cholesterol 0 mg

Preserved Peach

Preparation Time: 10 minutes
Cooking Time: 30 minutes
Serve: 16

Ingredients:

- 12 medium peaches
- 2 oz pectin
- 4 ½ cups sugar

Directions:

1. Crush 1 cup peaches in a large saucepan. Add remaining peaches into the saucepan and cook over medium-low heat. Bring to boil and cook for 20 minutes.
2. Add sugar and bring to boil over medium heat. Slowly add pectin and stir constantly for 1 minute.
3. Remove pan from heat.
4. Ladle peaches into the clean jars, leave ½-inch headspace. Remove air bubbles.
5. Seal jars with lids and process in a boiling water bath for 10 minutes.
6. Remove jars from the water bath and let it cool completely.
7. Check seals of jars. Label and store.

Nutritional Value (Amount per Serving):

- Calories 257
- Fat 0.3 g
- Carbohydrates 67 g
- Sugar 66.8 g
- Protein 1.1 g
- Cholesterol 0 mg

Strawberry Preserves

Preparation Time: 10 minutes
Cooking Time: 20 minutes
Serve: 10

Ingredients:

- 2 lbs strawberries
- 2 tbsp vinegar
- 5 cups sugar
- Pinch of salt

Directions:

1. Add all ingredients into the stockpot and bring to boil. Stir frequently and cook for 15-20 minutes.
2. Remove pot from heat.
3. Ladle strawberry preserves into the clean jars, leave ½-inch headspace. Remove air bubbles.
4. Seal jars with lids and process in a boiling water bath for 10 minutes.
5. Remove jars from the water bath and let it cool completely.
6. Check seals of jars. Label and store.

Nutritional Value (Amount per Serving):

- Calories 405
- Fat 0.3 g
- Carbohydrates 107 g
- Sugar 104.5 g
- Protein 0.6 g
- Cholesterol 0 mg

Chapter 13: Soup Recipes

Navy Bean Soup

Preparation Time: 10 minutes
Cooking Time: 1 hour 40 minutes
Serve: 12

Ingredients:

- 1 cup dried navy beans
- 1 1/2 cups carrot, sliced
- 3 cups ham, diced
- 4 cups chicken broth

Directions:

1. Add beans into the large bowl and cover with water. Cover and let sit for overnight.
2. Drain beans well. Add beans into the large pot and cover at least 2 inches of water. Bring to boil and simmer for 30 minutes.
3. Add broth to the saucepan and bring to boil.
4. Fill clean jars with an equal amount of carrots, ham, and beans. Top with hot broth. Leave 1-inch headspace.
5. Add lids and rings. Place jar into the pressure canner.
6. Process can soup pints for 75 minutes, quarts for 90 minutes at 10 lbs pressure in a pressure canner.
7. Check seals of jars. Label and store.

Nutritional Value (Amount per Serving):

- Calories 130
- Fat 3 g
- Carbohydrates 13 g
- Sugar 2 g
- Protein 11 g
- Cholesterol 20 mg

Tomato Soup

Preparation Time: 10 minutes
Cooking Time: 2 hours
Serve: 8

Ingredients:

- 7 lbs tomatoes, diced
- ½ tsp black pepper
- 1 tsp celery seed
- 2 tsp garlic, minced
- 2 bay leaves
- 2 tsp dried basil
- 1 tbsp dried oregano
- 3 tbsp brown sugar
- 3 tbsp tomato paste
- ½ cup water
- 1 cup onion, diced
- 1 ½ tsp salt

Directions:

1. Add onion and tomatoes in a large pot along with ½ cup water and cook for 30 minutes.
2. Remove pot from heat and puree the tomatoes using a blender until smooth.
3. Return tomato puree pot on heat. Add spices, herbs, sugar, and tomato paste. Stir well and bring to simmer for 60 minutes. Adjust salt.
4. Remove pot from heat. Add 1 tablespoon of lemon juice to each jar.
5. Fill a jar with soup. Leave 1/2 -inch headspace.
6. Seal jars with lids and process in a boiling water bath for 40 minutes.
7. Remove jars from the water bath and let it cool completely.
8. Check seals of jars. Label and store.

Nutritional Value (Amount per Serving):

- Calories 99
- Fat 1 g
- Carbohydrates 22 g
- Sugar 15 g
- Protein 4 g
- Cholesterol 0 mg

Canned Mushroom Soup

Preparation Time: 10 minutes
Cooking Time: 2 hours 20 minutes
Serve: 12

Ingredients:

- 6 cups baby Bella mushrooms, sliced
- 16 cups milk
- 2 cups tapioca starch
- 1 cup butter
- 4 tbsp sea salt

Directions:

1. Melt butter in a large saucepan over medium heat.
2. Add mushrooms and sauté for 5 minutes.
3. Add tapioca starch and salt and stir well. Slowly add milk and stir well.
4. Stir well and cook over medium heat until thickened.
5. Remove pan from heat. Ladle soup into the clean jars. Leave 1/2 –inch headspace.
6. Seal jars with lids and process in a boiling water bath for 2 hours.
7. Remove jars from the water bath and let it cool completely.
8. Check seals of jars. Label and store.

Nutritional Value (Amount per Serving):

- Calories 536
- Fat 37.5 g
- Carbohydrates 40.7 g
- Sugar 16.3 g
- Protein 12.1 g
- Cholesterol 108 mg

Carrot Soup

Preparation Time: 10 minutes
Cooking Time: 1 hour 35 minutes
Serve: 12

Ingredients:

- 4 lbs carrots, washed, peeled & sliced
- 1 lb fennel bulb, chopped
- 1 tsp dried thyme
- 2 tsp onion powder
- 12 cups vegetable stock
- 1 tbsp olive oil
- 1/2 tsp ground cumin
- 1 tsp ground black pepper
- 1 tsp ground coriander
- 1 tsp ground ginger
- 2 tbsp salt

Directions:

1. Heat oil in a saucepan over medium heat.
2. Add fennel and sauté until translucent.
3. Add carrots and 4 cups of stock and simmer for 30 minutes.
4. Remove saucepan from heat and using blender puree the carrots until smooth.
5. Return saucepan on heat.
6. Add remaining ingredients and stir well and cook on low heat for 20-30 minutes.
7. Ladle soup into the clean jars. Leave 1-inch headspace.
8. Seal jar with lids. Process in a water bath canner for 40 minutes.
9. Remove jars from the water bath and let it cool completely.
10. Check seals of jars. Label and store.

Nutritional Value (Amount per Serving):

- Calories 86
- Fat 1 g
- Carbohydrates 18 g
- Sugar 7 g
- Protein 2 g
- Cholesterol 0 mg

Celery Soup

Preparation Time: 10 minutes
Cooking Time: 30 minutes
Serve: 20

Ingredients:

- 1 lb celery, diced
- 1 onion, diced
- 4 cups vegetable stock
- 1 medium potato, peeled and diced
- 1 tbsp olive oil
- 1 garlic clove, minced
- ½ cup dry white wine

Directions:

1. Heat oil in a large pot over medium heat. Add onion, garlic, and celery and sauté until translucent, about 10 minutes. Add wine and stir well.
2. Add potato, stock, pepper, and salt, and simmer for 5 minutes.
3. Remove pot from heat.
4. Add lids and rings. Place jar into the pressure canner.
5. Process can soup for 10 minutes at 11 lbs pressure in a pressure canner.
6. Once done, cool canner, remove the lid and let jars stand for 10 minutes before removing from canner.
7. Remove carrots jars from canner and place them on the counter for 1-2 hours.
8. Check seals of jars. Label and store.

Nutritional Value (Amount per Serving):

- Calories 27
- Fat 1.2 g
- Carbohydrates 3.7 g
- Sugar 1.1 g
- Protein 0.5 g
- Cholesterol 0 mg

Conclusion

From soups and stews, to meals-in-a-jar, to kitchen staples like broths and beans, pressure canning is a time-honored craft that allows you to preserve the food your family loves to eat safely. With The Pressure Canning Cookbook For Beginners you will discover the ease of pressure canning, understand the science behind safe food preservation, and enjoy delicious recipes for stocking your kitchen and feeding your family.

The Pressure Canning Cookbook For Beginners not only offer you the necessary information but also provide alternative versions to take your canned food flavors up a notch. She will also provide recipes that highlight these unique flavor combinations so you can make use out of every canned.

Printed in the USA
CPSIA information can be obtained
at www.ICGtesting.com
LVHW010337091123
763484LV00005B/8